D1169372

Media Acclaim for *This is True*

"A tasty weekly collection."

John Higgins, *Net-Letter Guide*

"All the News That's Not Fit to Print."

Newsweek

"Best in Net Entertainment, 1994"

Eric Berlin, *Internet World*

"One of the most popular columns on the Internet."

QST

"The kind of news items that keep comedians and commentators in business."

Washington Post

"Two minutes after I subscribed... I was reading the current issue and chuckling."

Dave Farrell, *The Detroit News*

More Important: What our Readers Say . . . .

"Love what you're doing with the news. Nice to know somebody else is as demented as I. Keep it up."

George Tuck, Professor
College of Journalism and Mass Communications
University of Nebraska/Lincoln

"I am a teacher of English as a foreign language at West Fjords Junior College. I use your material in my classroom: each story is concise and to the point. Your subtle use of language is also a big factor."

Gudjon Olafsson, Teacher
Isafjordur, Iceland

"How can I describe it? Witty, bizarre, cutting, and very useful might do. *This is True* is superb."

Ed Ricketts, Features Editor
.net magazine, Bath, England

"The one about the Bleeping Idiot [Jan. 1] is priceless. Price-**less!!** *Unübertroffen!* ['cannot be surpassed']"

Jan Dreier, Writer
Venice, Calif.

"As crazy as the world is, it's always fun to look at society with a smile and a laugh. *True* does this without losing its cerebral quality, which is quite an accomplishment!"

Jeremy M. Helfgot, President
JMH Media, Los Angeles, Calif.

"I love it and my wife likes it even better. She can't wait to get her hands on it every week."

Dick Rowden, USAF (Retired)
San Antonio, Texas

"I spend about half my time on the road, much of it in Russia and the other former Soviet republics. My ability to access *True* in the CIS brings much good cheer. When I am travelling with a group, my laptop becomes the center of life one evening a week while everyone reads *This is True!*"

Max B. Flaxman, President
Grynberg Resources Inc., Cranford N.J.

"I find *This is True* relaxing: it's filled with strange, bizarre and mostly funny material, not to mention your comments (I like them)."

Igor Urbiha, Teaching Assistant
Zagreb, Croatia

"Thanks for your service to humanity. Can you be knighted?"

Atish Sanyal, Information Officer
Washington, D.C.

This Is True:
Deputy Kills Man With Hammer
And 500 Other Bizarre-but-*True* Stories
and Headlines from the World's Press

The *This Is True* Collection, Volume One

This Is True:

Deputy Kills Man With Hammer
And 500 Other Bizarre-but-*True* Stories
and Headlines from the World's Press

The *This Is True* Collection, Volume One

by

Randy Cassingham

Freelance Communications
Pasadena, California

Published by Freelance Communications
  Post Office Box 91970
  Pasadena, California, 91109 USA
  (500) 448-TRUE (448-8783) • Fax (500) 442-TRUE (442-8783)

Printed and bound in the United States of America using
  non-petroleum ink on acid-free paper.

9 8 7 6 5 4 3 2 1

Library of Congress Catalog Card Number: 95-61330

International Standard Book Number: 0-935309-21-7

For my Parents:

Larry, who inspired in me a curiosity about
    virtually all things, and
Marge, who inspired in me an appreciation
    for the arts.

...What an enriching combination.

Freelance Communications' books are available in quantity at discount to companies, clubs and other organizations. Contact us for details.

Lost track of Freelance Communications? If we've moved since this book was published, you'll always be able to find our current address in *Books in Print,* which can be found in most any book store or library.

Edited by Robert Nelson
Author Photograph by Gary Kapich
Book and Cover Design by Freelance Communications

Introduction . . . .

I've known Randy Cassingham since 1987, when he and
I both showed up at a meeting about the interface
designs for the operational systems on the U.S. space
station, which is what I was working on at the time. As
the people around the table talked, I noticed that he sat
leaning back in his chair, listening intently, his note pad
remaining blank. He didn't say a word except in two
types of situations: to point out when someone said
something that was inconsistent with what they had
said earlier, or to blurt out an ironic one-liner that was
both funny and instructive.
The one that I remember best happened during a heated
discussion of when the "PDR" was going to finalize the

**Randy tends to see things in a different light, picking
the weird out of a bunch of mundane, seemingly unrelated
details, and making some comment about it that is
ironic, hilarious, twisted, attention-getting, bizarre, or an
incredibly sick sexual double entendré — and more often
than might be expected, all of the above.**

"WBS" for the "ELM" or whatever. Randy's voice
stopped the exchange, partly because he hadn't talked
much and people were a little startled, and partly for
what he said: "We need to watch out for excessive TLAs."
The people around the table looked at each other: TLAs...
TLAs? and glanced at their notes to see if they could
figure out what that meant. "Three-Letter Acronyms,"
Randy explained, dropping the other shoe. It was a
low-key but effective way to make an important point:
the language of the discussion was getting so convoluted
that it was becomming unclear what was going on, even
to the experienced NASA system designers and human
factors engineers there. Not too smart when astronauts'
lives might ultimately depend on decisions made by the
people in the room.

Since I'm no fan of the bureaucratic mindset myself, I knew this guy would be a longtime friend. It was obvious that we shared a similar sense of humor, and I've found that what people laugh at lets you know what they think is really important. Not that Randy tells good jokes (which he *can* do, occasionally), but that he tends to see things in a different light, picking the weird out of a bunch of mundane, seemingly unrelated details, and making some comment about it that is ironic, hilarious, twisted, attention-getting, bizarre, or an incredibly sick sexual double entendré — and, more often than might be expected, all of the above.

Don't get me wrong: it's not Robin Williamsesque, it's not constant, but all of the sudden you realize what he has just said, rather quietly and out-of-the-blue, and it knocks you over by the insight it expresses.

After I took a job across the country, we would write each other occasionally. Usually, he would throw in a wild newspaper clipping or six. On each of the clips, parts would be highlighted in yellow, and, in Randy's block printing in red in the margin, there would be a comment that made you realize how absurd people can be. Like the lady who kept a .38 caliber revolver under her pillow, next to her asthma inhaler. One night, while having an asthma attack, she grabbed the wrong item, stuck it in her mouth and pulled the trigger (Randy's comment, of course, was "There she goes, shooting her mouth off again.")

I'm not the only one that was blessed with the little bits of paper that would fall out of the envelope when it was opened. He had several correspondents like me, and he would sometimes have to copy the gems for each of us. But they were still all individually highlighted and commented in his red felt pen.

On a business trip a couple of years ago, I visited Randy at his "day job" workplace. His office area was a partitioned cubicle among many others on a main hall, and on the outside of his wall hung a bulletin board (for you teenagers out there: not a computer with a modem, but a cork board that things are attached to with thumb tacks!) And there, posted for the passersby in the building, were the same articles — only there were more of them than *I* ever got. But not because they were piling up: there were several pages of *recent* stories there, all highlighted in yellow and commented in red.

When I expressed amazement as to all of the articles he had up there, he confessed that he was actually holding back: he picked up his briefcase and pulled out several *more* pages of clippings. "Watch this," he said, and he walked out and replaced the pages on the board with new ones. In his usual not-very-loud voice, he called out to the people in the adjoining cubicles: "new clippings going up!" and slipped back into his office. I doubted that anyone had heard him, but several cubicles away, someone said "new clippings?", and a moment later there were a couple of rows of people clustered around the board, all wanting to see the latest from the human interest newsfront.

Back hidden with me behind the wall of his own cubicle, Randy whispered to me "where do you *get* this stuff?", which left me saying "huh?", but sure enough, about 12 seconds later, one woman reading the board yelled over the partition, laughing: "where do you *get* this stuff?", which left Randy with a "what did I tell you" smirk on his face — and left me rolling on the floor!

And where indeed? A lot of it isn't that the story itself is bizarre — so often it is a plain old news story with some weird detail buried eight paragraphs down. But Randy pulls out that detail, pointing to it with that yellow highlighter. Quite often, the irony of the item doesn't hit you until you read Randy's comment. It may be a little sick, but I think maybe it's also a gift.

I'm not the only one that urged Randy to write a column, but he didn't want to be tied down, required to "fill newspaper columns or else." But his clips were passed around by his friends, and people wanted more. It finally got to the point where it was taking too much time for him to copy, and highlight, and mark them all with red.

Luckily for all of us who needed our twisted news fix, the worldwide Internet computer network, which was just about to explode into mass popularity at that time, enabled the clips to become e-mail, and they started

flashing around to his friends. And they started going to his friends' friends, who would e-mail him and say "as long as you're e-mailing these anyway, can you put me on the distribution list too?", until the e-mail distribution list got so big that he moved the whole operation over to an Internet e-mail "list server" and allowed *anyone* to "subscribe" to his clippings, with the computer doing all the work of keeping track of who needed copies. Even though it was free, he did it formally and professionally, because, he told me, they were "going out to strangers, and I don't want to make a bad impression."
And that's how "This is True" was born*.

Of course, it wasn't long until newspapers wanted into the act, and *"True"* started appearing in print, and now Randy is required to "fill newspaper columns or else." (Which serves him right!)

True still goes to tens of thousands of people around the world by e-mail every week. But how does he pay the considerable expense of that? By gathering up the columns and publishing a book of them. At least I *hope* this volume brings in some bucks — please buy several extra copies and give them to friends. They'll be amply entertained, and you'll make it that much more likely that Randy can continue to send me my e-mail fix every week. And when I say "please," I mean *please* — I'm addicted.

John J. Bosley, Ph.D.
Montgomery Village, Md.

---

* For the first several months, it was known on the 'net as "This Just In".

Preface . . . .

Welcome to the the first *This is True* collection. *This is True* is a weekly collection of bizarre-but-true news items with running commentary, plus a true "headline of the week", that is sold to newspapers and magazines as a feature column. I like pulling out the weird, the bizarre, the amazing things that humans do in real life, and then putting my own spin on them.

Luckily, I don't have to recount the story of how *True* got started (thanks, John, for your great Introduction — you could always tell the long stories better than I). Once it became available on the Internet, it caught on pretty fast. The list of subscribers grew at the rate of 20 per week — for two weeks. Then, it caught on like wildfire

---

I like pulling out the weird, the bizarre, the amazing things that humans do in real life, and then putting my own spin on them.

— I thought — and subscriptions started coming in at the rate of 40–50 *per day,* slowing down only slightly each weekend.

Then, press coverage started: *Newsweek* wrote it up, giving out my e-mail address. *Internet World* called it "the best in Net entertainment" for the year. And, of course, online "zines" and mainstream newspapers started doing items on it, and subscriptions started to come in by the *hundreds* every day. By the end of the first year, the total e-mail readership was estimated to have reached six figures — not to mention the readers of print publications ranging from the tiny *Ft. Nelson News* on the Alaska Highway in British Columbia, Canada, to the popular *Hemmets Journal* in Malmö, Sweden.

But let's pull back a bit: what is it I mean by "true"? *True*'s stories don't come from the tabloids or underground newspapers — they come from the legitimate/mainstream media, such as regular news wires, city newspapers, and major newsweeklies like *Newsweek.* Very rarely, stories from other printed sources will be used if I'm quite convinced that the event described really happened.

But let me caution you: take *everything* you read in newspapers — and even *This is True* — with at least a small grain of salt. In addition to my job as a writer, I've worked a few other careers, including a brief stint as a sheriff deputy, several years as a paramedic, and quite a while working at a large facility of a major U.S. government space agency, whom I suspect may not want to claim me, so I'll omit their name. But the one thing in common in all of these jobs is that I have often been a participant in events that tend to end up on the news or in the paper. And not *once,* when I knew the full story, did any news report on the event come without some error in the "facts". So I watch carefully for corrections. Whenever I've discovered that an item in *This is True* was based on a "fact" taken in error, or indeed if I've made an error myself, the item has been corrected. But I have resisted the temptation to improve (beyond grammar or typos) my comments — they are as they were written under deadline pressure.

You'll be happy to note that even if you've read *This is True* every week from the very beginning, you still have *not* read every story in this book. I very often have leftovers which don't fit in the weekly column (it *does* have a word limit). Some weeks have them, some don't, but there are more than 100 of them mixed in throughout, plus a section of leftover headlines. If there's one thing I've learned over the years, it's that there is never a shortage of material about the weird things we humans do.

Randy Cassingham
Pasadena, California
July 1995

Author's Note Regarding Sources . . . .

The stories for *This is True* come from "legitimate" printed news media, both American and international (see more in my preface). I try as much as possible to credit the *original* source. For example, if a story is taken from a newspaper, but the newspaper credits a wire service as the source, I do too — I don't necessarily credit the paper I found the story in. Thus the most-cited sources in this book are the major news wires:

- AP (Associated Press)
- Reuter (Reuters Ltd.)
- UPI (United Press International)

Other sources were also used, and are identified in parentheses at the end of each story, before my comment, just as the above sources are.

"News is the first rough draft of history."

Philip L. Graham (1915–63)
Publisher, *Washington Post*

26 June 1994 . . . .

Heeeeeee Did It: The Appeal Court in Great Britain has been asked to review a murder conviction on the basis that the jury reached its verdict after a seance — which would mean they did not reach their verdict solely based on evidence presented in court, as required. It seems three of the jurors used a Ouija Board to contact the murder victim, who pointed his phantom finger at Stephen Young, 35, as the culprit. The 12-person jury went on to convict Young unanimously. (Reuter) ...*Maybe we can get Daniel Webster for the defense.*

Rubbed The Wrong Way: Having one of his regular massages in downtown Jakarta, Indonesia, Pradikto Suratno, 59, ended up having sex with his masseuse, a Ms. Wiwiek, 36. In the middle of the *...uh...* act, Ms. Wiwiek became aware that Mr. Suratno wasn't moving anymore — indeed, he had stopped breathing and was dead. She wriggled out from underneath him, and police were called. Officers confiscated the dead man's clothing and the massage cream as "evidence". The Jakarta Post ran a story on the matter, delicately headlined "Man Dies in the Saddle". (Reuter) ...*I wonder how she could tell he was dead, and not just being himself?*

April Showers Bring May Bills: Neil Davis, whose car rental firm in Yorkshire, England is housed in a 12 x 8 foot office, recently received a 62-pound (US$94) water bill from Yorkshire Water. Sounds reasonable, except the office has no water connections, nor drains. When he called to complain, he was told the bill was for drainage of water that rained onto his roof. Are they kidding? he asked. "We are certainly not." However, the disputed bill is on hold pending an investigation as to whether the rain drains down onto open land, or whether it's going down the drain, which would allow the bill to be enforced. (Reuter) ...*Wait until the BBC finds out that their TV signals are penetrating his walls, yet he isn't paying for them.*

Bill Who? In early June, the Newsweek Poll surveyed Americans as to whom they consider "role models" for young people, based on "what you know about their character". The Reverend Billy Graham "won", with 64% agreeing he is a good to excellent role model. General Colin Powel was close behind with 60%. The top woman: Hillary Clinton (48%). Interestingly, President Clinton came in just *behind* Dan Quayle, with only 40% and 44%, respectively, agreeing they were good to excellent role models. (Newsweek) *...C'mon Dan, you can tell me: what's your secret? I'll let you sit in the Big Chair for a minute. Please?*

I Thought They Just Tossed Pea Soup: Anthony Dearinger, a preacher at the Independent Baptist Church in Hillsboro, Ill., demonstrated this spring how God will pitch the Devil into hell on Judgment Day by picking up a 12-year-old boy from the pews where he was sitting with his parents and throwing him six feet. Dearinger was convicted of child endangerment in May. (AP) *...Good thing the sermon wasn't about crucifixion.*

It's OK — It's a Documentary: The BBC paid Tony and Wendy Duffield of London 12,000 pounds (US$18,000) to have sex for a TV documentary. Easy, except for when you consider where the cameras were: she had a $23,000 camera fitted inside her vagina, he had a camera strapped to his penis. The footage, intended to capture the act of lovemaking from an *...uh...* inside point of view, required 63 sessions of strenuous effort by the couple over a period of three weeks. (Reuter) *...Again? In that case, call in my stunt double.*

Desperate Measures: Steve Marek, a hypnotist in Frankfort, Ky., ran a newspaper advertisement advising women that he could help enlarge their breasts "one full cup size without surgery or implants, safely, through hypnosis with a program developed by a medical doctor." The state's attorney general wasn't amused, and sued the therapist on a charge of deceptive business practices. Marek told investigators that he "performed the technique on two friends about a year ago, but only as a personal favor." (AP) *...I'll just lay my hands on you, and you will be **healed**!!*

Let Us Know When You Decide
NY Ponders Beating Victim
AP headline

---

3 July 1994 . . . .

The Shirts Off Their Backs: In an annual event, nudists in Texas are celebrating National Nude Week (week of July 3) by donating spare clothing to Texas charities. Linda Krabill, manager of the 700-member Live Oak Nudist Ranch, says nudism is the most "egalitarian form of recreation" in that "nudity is a great leveling experience. When a person isn't wearing an Armani suit, you don't know that he's a surgeon." (UPI) *...Have you ever met a surgeon who hasn't wanted to advertise the fact? But then again, I'd rather see a nude surgeon than one in an Armani suit.*

Liquor Really is Quicker: Despite the well-known fact that alcohol consumption depresses sexual ability in men, alcohol has long been used by men as an aid to seduce women, apparently because it works. Finnish and Japanese researchers now think they know why: alcohol apparently causes women's bodies to produce testosterone, the "male" sex hormone that is involved in female arousal. (Reuter) *...Finnish and Japanese researchers? ("You try hot sake, we'll try the sauna. Whoever goes all the way first wins.")*

Slap Happy, Go Lucky: Akira Koike, a freelance film critic travelling in Manila, the Philippines, was arrested and charged with "slander-by-deed" when he objected to a $49 charge for extra baggage by slapping Northwest Airlines staff supervisor Tiam Beng. How does one get out of such a predicament? Koike got on his knees at Beng's feet and begged forgiveness. Beng accepted his apologies and prosecutors ordered him set free. (Reuter) *...Awwww. Can't we whack him with a rattan cane at least once?*

Desperately Needs a Hobby: Terry Grice, 26, of Jackson County, Fla., celebrated a bout of depression by building a wooden rig to hold his penis and testicles in place while he used a circular saw to cut them off. He then tossed the dismembered parts into the back of his pickup truck and drove 50 miles to a hospital in Alabama for medical care. For days, Grice insisted that he had been attacked by strangers, but finally admitted that he had done the deed himself. His wife, three stepchildren and a nephew slept through the incident. (Reuter) *...And presto! No more unsightly bulge!*

Reach Out and Touch Someone: Maybe this somehow explains all the charges of extramarital affairs and sexual harassment. "Meeting him, shaking his hand — it was overwhelming. It was better than sex. Of course, I haven't had sex before, but I'm sure this was better," said Tyler Peterson, high school student/Boys Nation delegate, after meeting President Clinton last year. Then Judith Krantz, author of "Scruples" and other fine American books, recently said "Shaking hands with Bill Clinton is, in and of itself, a full-body sexual experience, I promise you. He has the sexiest handshake of any man that I have ever experienced in my life." (Quotes from Newsweek) *...I feel sorry for the kid, but Judy should know better by now!*

Reach Out and Touch Someone II: A woman in Devizes, southern England, was awakened in the early morning hours by a telephone call. Hearing moaning, she thought it was an obscene call and hung up. When the phone rang again, bringing similar noises, she was about to hang up again until she recognized her daughter's voice, yelling "Oh my God!" and followed by a man's voice. Sure her daughter was being attacked at her home, mom called police, who sped to the scene to find the daughter quite willingly being *...uh...* friendly with the man in her bedroom. In the throes of passion, the couple apparently accidentally pressed the "redial" button on the phone with their toes, connecting the boudoir to mom. "This is a warning for other people — if you're going to indulge in this sort of thing, move the phone," a police spokesman said. (Reuter) *...or at least put **my** number on your autodialer.*

News To Us
Wrecks Blamed On Carelessness
AP headline

---

10 July 1994 . . . .

Line of Duty: New York City police officer Carol Shaya posed nude for Playboy magazine, and is now facing department disciplinary charges. Because she posed nude? Not exactly: police spokesman John Miller said she might be charged with failing to file a proper "off-duty work" form, wearing her uniform in some of the photos, and using the department's name for personal gain. The work form Shaya submitted stated the work was for sportswear modelling. It is reported that Shaya earned $75,000 for her layout. (AP) *...I'm sure the definition of "sport" is loose enough that she can beat the rap.*

You Are What You Eat: Christopher Lyons, a drug dealer serving time in prison, filed a $310,000 lawsuit against the Kellogg Co., claiming that a "defective" Pop Tart injured his mouth and caused him nightmares, which lead to 72 hours of sleep deprivation. U.S. District Judge Benjamin Gibson dismissed the suit, saying there was no proof of suffering worth at least $50,000, the minimum for a federal lawsuit — partly, the judge noted, because Lyons had lost no wages and incurred no medical expenses. (AP) *...But your honor: I easily earned $50,000 in 72 hours on the outside!*

Those Who Can, Do: A university professor in Bologna, Italy, writing a paper on the sociology of love, checked his local library for books on kissing. Finding none in Italian, the library arranged for the interlibrary loan of four scholarly books on the subject — from Yorkshire England. When the Yorkshire librarian called the Italian librarian to ask why the reputedly great-loving Italians didn't have any academic books on such a basic topic, they retorted "Because we are far too busy doing it to write about it." (Reuter) *...But the professor seems to have plenty of time to write.*

Really Did get the Wrong Guy: Claude A. Smith, 60, a black man housed in an Ohio prison, was in need of prostate surgery. Claude E. Smith III, 43, a white man who until recently was housed in another Ohio prison, is suing the state of Ohio for $3 million, claiming his prostate was removed in error when they sent for the wrong Claude Smith. He charges the operation left him impotent and without bladder control. (AP) *...Don't ever get your second opinion from a guard.*

Apparently Didn't See the Movie: A Universal Studios Hollywood employee — an unnamed woman who normally works weekdays in the wardrobe department —

discovered while leaving work on a recent Saturday that her regular exit gate was locked. Driving around the lot looking for escape, she started to follow a tour bus full of visitors, presumably figuring it would lead her to an exit. The bus then cut through the special passageway that was used to film Charlton Heston leading the Israelites through the parted waters of the Red Sea, and the woman followed. But upon reaching the end, the bus triggered a device to close the parted waters, trapping the woman and her car, much like the Pharaoh's soldiers were trapped when they chased Heston and company through the gap. It took Hollywood's Urban Search and Rescue unit an hour to rescue her. (LA Times) ...*Better than being caught in King Kong's grasp for an hour, I suppose.*

The American Way: Paul Siemens, 18, of Chestnut Ridge, N.Y., graduated second in his class from Spring Valley High School. Despite having been accepted at Harvard to study biology, he has filed suit against the school district, calling their method of determining class rank "erroneous, arbitrary and capricious", and claiming that he would have been number one based on straight grade point average. The suit demands that he be made class valedictorian because in the future, graduate school entrance and grant awards will take his high school class rank into account, and he would be placed at a disadvantage by being ranked number two. (AP) ...*Biology? But he clearly would make a gifted lawyer.*

Mamma Said you were No Good
Death Row Inmate Seeks Divorce
AP headline

---

17 July 1994 . . . .

Long Arm of the Law: When Douglas Murphy bolted past the courtroom of Municipal Judge Donald Hoover and ran out the door, the Richland County (Ohio) judge knew what he had to do: he dropped his robe and ran after him. During the 20-minute chase, a team of roofers helped point the way for the judge and several police officers who had joined in the pursuit. Like his late namesake, Hoover got his man, finding Murphy hiding behind a bush. He's not likely to get any awards, though: Murphy wasn't an escapee, but had just finished a court appearance and was hurrying away, free on bond. (AP) ..."*Of all escape mechanisms, death is the most efficient.*" —H.L. Mencken.

Equal Treatment: "Male rape" wasn't illegal in Britain until this week, when the upper house of parliament passed a law that provides an equivalent maximum penalty for female rape: life. Previously, the only charges that could be brought were sexual assault or "non-consensual buggery", which provided for a maximum 10-year sentence. The Reuter news service points out that the action "follows a vote earlier this year by parliament to lower the age of consent for male homosexuals from 21 to 18." ...*In other words, "easy come, easy go"?*

Parton's Body, Reagan's Head, Schwarzenegger's Disposition: According to Federal charges filed in Charleston, W. Va., businessman Denny Ray Gullett sent his partner, Masel Hensley, a gift, telling him he "would get a bang out of" it. Prosecutors say it was filled with dynamite. Hensley's son was killed in the blast, and a nephew — the unwitting delivery man — severely injured. The intended victim had a $150,000 insurance policy on his life, with the company as beneficiary. Gullett allegedly had told the nephew the box contained a blow-up doll with Dolly Parton's body and Ronald Reagan's head. (AP) ...*A product, no doubt, advertised as having three boobs.*

Consider This a Divorce: Mary Stiles says her husband, Grady, 55, a sideshow performer who went by the name "Lobster Boy" because of a genetic deformity which left him with ...*well*... lobster-claw-like hands, beat her and their children so severely that she had no other choice but to hire the next-door neighbor to shoot him. Since Stiles had been convicted for the 1978 murder of one of his daughter's boyfriends and then released on probation, she believed him when he said he would kill her if she filed for divorce. The neighbor was convicted of murder and conspiracy, and sentenced to 27 years. (AP) ...*at 55, shouldn't he have been called "Lobster Man"?*

Weird Relationships II: Carol Cieslak charged her boy-friend, Dennis Amber, 44, with assault, saying he had reacted to their breakup by coming over to her house with a snapping turtle, which he tried to get to bite her. But Cieslak dropped the charges in the Coraopolis, Pa. court because media coverage of the assault "has made her life hell," the judge said. (AP) ...*Maybe Amber should get a new job. I hear there's a sideshow performer position open.*

They're Professionals — Don't Try This at Home: District Court Judge Daniel Sawicki had had enough: Gregory Wright, 22, in court charged with assault with intent to murder in the shooting of a Royal Oak, Mich. police officer, continually chanted "Please don't kill me" during his ar-raignment. Despite orders from the judge to keep quiet, Wright kept chanting. So, on orders from the judge, court officers taped his mouth shut with duct tape, wrapping it around his head several times. (AP) ...*And quit squirming or we'll pinch your nose.*

Really Know how to Party: Four men, ranging in ages from 18 to 21, celebrated a long night of drinking and drugs by apparently deciding to lie down between the rails as a train passed over them. But a 144-car Norfolk Southern freight train made such a mess of them, authorities had to search for several hours to find one of their heads. "It appears ...they may have thought the train was high enough to pass over them," said Prince William County (Va.) Common-wealth's Attorney Paul B. Ebert. It wasn't. (AP) ...*Next week: wing walking on a 747.*

I'll See You After School: Debi Mercer, 42, the wife of the Yamhill County (Ore.) district attorney, pleaded guilty last week to charges of sexual abuse and official misconduct when it was discovered that she had kissed a 14-year-old boy she was supervising in school detention. The boy, who is now 16, told investigators that the two had engaged in sexual relations both on and off school grounds for the past two years, and that she had performed oral sex on him. In a plea bargained sentence, Mercer avoided jail time but is on 30 days' house arrest, five years' probation, must pay $2,500 for psychological therapy for the boy, and must stay away from boys under 18. (AP) ...*Surely a 42-year-old man caught with a 14-year-old girl would have been Bobbitized.*

Not a Bad Idea
Ex-lawmaker Remains Chained to Statue
UPI headline

24 July 1994 . . . .

Opposites Attract: It has been recently revealed that Vickie Lynn Hogan Smith, 26, better known as supermodel Anna Nicole Smith (poser for Guess? Jeans ads and Playboy magazine), married J. Howard Marshall II, 89, a Houston, Tex. oilman. Smith has recently appeared in the film "Naked Gun 33-1/3" while Marshall recently appeared in Forbes magazine's list of the 400 richest people in the U.S. ($550 million in 1991). Meanwhile, Smith is the defendant in a lawsuit — her child's nanny accuses her of sexual harassment, sexual assault and false imprisonment. Smith has countersued for slander. (AP) ...*Slander? For saying Smith sleeps with old men or something?*

Bad Press is Better than No Press? The Kansas City (Mo.) chapter of the Public Relations Society of America is sponsoring a contest, circulating a pamphlet to solicit entries. The pamphlet uses a Nazi swastika on the cover as an example of attention-grabbing public relations, with the slogan "Never Underestimate The Driving Force of Public Relations". A spokesman for the PR firm that created the graphic for the association says the brochure was meant to be "provocative". So far, it has provoked at least one PR firm to drop out of the awards competition. (AP) ...*Next year, let's let Saddam Hussein Images, Inc., produce the brochure.*

Gold in That Thar Country: The government of China has decided to let foreign firms invest in gold mining operations there, but only in mines that are difficult to get gold out of: those that produce less than 3.5 grams of glitter per ton of ore. And "according to the rules," said the Chinese official news agency, all gold produced is to "be sold to the People's Bank of China at the state-set price." (Reuter) ...*Or, "We get the gold, the investors get the shaft."*

Peek-a-booth: David K. Paro, the owner of a combination tanning salon and video store in Buffalo, Mo., was charged with using a hidden camera to make videotapes of under-age girls. Police found tapes of at least 83 nude women, but didn't bring charges against him because Missouri has no laws against secret taping. But when some of the subjects turned out to be under the age of 18, the case came under the state's child abuse laws. Paro now faces 70 years in prison and a $50,000 fine. "I wasn't really doing it for money or the thrill — it was just sort of a prank, you know. It was just to see if it could be done," Paro said. (AP) ...*And the DA wants to push for the maximum sentence, just to see if it can be done.*

A Woman's Work is Never Done: Marie Hynes, 73, saw in her newspaper that her former husband, John Gonsalves Sr., 71, had won $5.1 million in the Massachusetts state lottery. Hynes "deserves" some of the booty, she says, and has filed a claim in family court asking for back child support for their three sons through the age of 21 and unspecified alimony. Gonsalves had left her in 1946; their youngest child is 51. He will receive $170,000 per year until the year 2013. (AP) ...*At least she doesn't hold a grudge.*

Buck the System: Jeremiah Johnson appeared in court in Polk County (Fla.), but the bailiff told him he couldn't wear shorts in front of the judge. So Johnson went out, took them off, and came back in. "He was butt naked," Judge Michael Raiden said later. "He was making a statement, I guess." The judge made a statement too: 179 days in jail for contempt of court. (AP) ...*I thought justice was supposed to be blind.*

Lord, Give me Strength — and a New Medial Meniscus: Researchers at the University of Southampton (England) have found that constant kneeling in prayer can cause arthritis of the knees. The study of 2,000 people found that excessive kneeling strains the knee, increasing wear of its cartilage. Most at risk are vicars, priests and nuns, the study said. (Reuter) ...*While you're down there, ask for money to pay for joint replacement surgery.*

Thief Blows it: A thief snatched a bag from a train in Reading, west of London, England, but paused after he got outside the station to look inside. He found enough explosives to make several bombs — he had apparently ripped off a terrorist group. He ran away, screaming, "It's a bomb, it's a bomb!" Scotland Yard's anti-terrorist team disposed of the explosives, while a witness observed, "I think he'll think twice about nicking bags that aren't his again." (Reuter) ...*The witness originally thought the guy had found a videotape of "Last Action Hero".*

Reminds me of When we First Met: The Nike sportswear company has won a temporary sales ban in Britain against two Spanish firms from marketing a perfume called "Nike", saying customers would assume it was made by the shoe company. A trial will determine whether the ban should be made permanent. (Reuter) ...*Yes, I like women who smell like gym shoes.*

Well, We Wondered about the Little Moustache: Ted Ridings, 79, was touring the British Museum when he spotted two stone faces, billed as 2000-year-old "Celtic carvings". But he remembered that his brother, Leslie, had carved the stone heads in 1939, making them to resemble Benito Mussolini and Adolf Hitler. Embarrassed museum officials removed the carvings from the exhibit. (Reuter) ...*Now, about that ancient "Walkman" found at Stonehenge....*

Didn't Want to Waste a Bullet
Deputy Kills Man With Hammer
AP headline

---

31 July 1994 . . . .

Save the Wails: To protect sea turtle hatchlings making their way to the surf from their dry-land nests, the U.S. Fish and Wildlife Service has ordered vehicles off the beaches in Daytona Beach, Fla., between the hours of 8:00 a.m. and 7:00 p.m. But local residents are in an uproar, saying that the economy of the beach area needs the daytime traffic to survive. "I'm sick and tired of tree-huggers and Bambi-ites," said George Locke, a member of the Beach Trust Commission, a county advisory board. "I like turtles, I used to eat them before they were protected," he said. Fish and Game officials threaten to close the beaches entirely during the turtles' mating season if the county doesn't do more to safeguard the hatchlings, which are protected under the Endangered Species Act. (AP) *...Hey, you got any more of them Bald Eagle-kabobs?*

We Secretly Substituted: Suspicious of the taste of the company coffee, employees of the Wire Rope of America company in St. Joseph, Mo., set up a secret camera. The resulting tape showed an employee who was "feuding" with other employees was using the pot as *...well...* a pot: he was using it as a urinal. Not to worry, said the Kansas City health director: "A healthy person normally puts out relatively noninfectious urine," though "from the aesthetic point of view, it's gross." (AP) *...and now **all** of the employees are pissed off.*

Life's a Crapshoot: In lieu of wedding gifts, a couple in London, England, is asking that guests instead place bets with a bookmaker in their name. If the bet pays, the couple will collect the winnings. "If not, we will still have a lot of fun," the groom said. (Reuter) *...I put $500 down 10:1 that you would be divorced in a year. Good luck!*

Call Me Romantic: Another Brit couple didn't even make it to the altar: Bill Langley's fiancee Barbara called the wedding off, but he had already booked a two-week honeymoon trip to Barbados. Not wanting to waste it, he advertised for someone "feminine" to take Barbara's place on the trip. While *...uh...* consummation wouldn't be required, "it is a honeymoon and it would be lovely if we got close," he said. So far, 50 women have applied for the position. (Reuter) *...Great scam idea! Get me my travel agent!!*

Turn Your Head and Cough: In a bizarre twist in a bizarre case, M. William Graybill, the judge presiding over the case of the Florida woman accused in the murder of "Lobster Boy", her allegedly abusive husband who was employed as a carnival performer [17 July], has come down with tuberculosis, and 18 others in the courthouse have also tested positive for the disease. Another judge took over the case, who promptly reversed Graybill's ruling that the woman could not claim self-defense in the case as an abused wife. The woman was found guilty of murder this week. (Reuter) *...Can a "movie of the week" be far behind?*

Charrrrrge! Five-hundred reserves from the Irish army were sent to the hospital when, apparently caught up in the heat of battle, they got a little carried away and suffered cuts, bruises, sunstroke and dehydration. But it wasn't a war: they were performing as extras in Mel Gibson's latest film, "Braveheart", being shot in England. "The Irish Reserve Army don't see much real action, so this could be the only chance they'll ever have," a military spokesman explained. (Reuter) *...I love the smell of single-malt in the morning.*

Teach them to Snort while they're Young: Consumer advocates are urging the ban of "Magic Scent" Crayolas — crayons with aroma capsules built into their wax — because the scents might entice children to eat them. Company officials insist that the crayons themselves don't have much scent, but when used the aroma capsules burst and "only the pictures" smell, a company spokesman said. But then, some kids will be enticed to lick or eat the paper, retorted the director of a poison control center. (AP) *...Apparently, these guys have never seen what kids put in their mouths. Crayons would probably be better for them.*

Are You Working or Attending this Convention? The World Health Organization and the European Commission invited the Scottish Prostitutes Education Project, a self-help group run since 1986 by and for *...well...* professional women, to stage a three-day conference focusing on health issues related to prostitution. "This self-help group has achieved a reputation as a world-wide center of excellence," said Martin Plant, a consultant to the World Health Organization and a professor at Edinburgh University. He is also the Project's vice-chairman. (Reuter) *...Ah, the world's second oldest profession: capitalizing on the honorable practitioners of the world's first oldest profession.*

Peace on Earth: The State Attorney of Ohio vows to appeal a federal court ruling which allows the Ku Klux Klan to display a cross at the Ohio Statehouse at Christmas. The state had argued not that the display would offend anyone, but that allowing it might give the impression that the state was endorsing Christianity in violation of the separation of church and state. (AP) *...That's what I hate about the holidays now: they're getting so commercial.*

Please — the term is "Emotionally Challenged"

Scientists Claim Mad Cow Disease Breakthrough

Reuter headline

---

7 August 1994 . . . .

Turf Wars: Prostitutes in Central Falls, R.I., were so incensed at a rival gang of hookers imported from Massachusetts that they called the police on them. After the two imports were arrested, the local ladies led the cops to their pimp, who was also arrested. "They'll rat each other out in a second. Drug dealers and prostitutes. It's unbelievable," said the local police chief. (AP) *...These small towns are sure protective of their local businesses.*

Driver's License Continued on Page Two: Antony Hicks, 23, of Turo, England, likes the rock group "Level 42". A lot. So he changed his name to reflect the names of all of the band's records and original members. Hicks, now legally known as "Ant Level Forty Two The Pursuit Of Accidents The Early Tapes Standing In The Light True Colours A Physical Presence World Machine Running in the Family Running In The Family Platinum Edition Staring At The Sun Level Best Guaranteed The Remixes Forever Now Influences Changes Mark King Mike Lindup Phil Gould Boon Gould Wally Badarou Lindup-Badarou," only told his wife of the change after it was recorded in court. (Reuter) *...Yes, very well. And your last name, sir?*

Oh, Crap! Alexander Perez, 19, of Maracaibo, Venezuela, got an urgent call from nature. Seeking privacy in a nearby animal's cage, he had his pants down to his knees when the occupant of the pen, a lion, took offense at his presence and attacked him. Perez struggled both to live and to get his pants up; a friend helped by hitting the lion with a brick. (Reuter) *...and that brick came from ...where?*

Doubting Tony: Church of England vicar Anthony Freeman lost his license to preach Sunday for writing a book last year in which he questioned the literal existence of God and the

Holy Trinity. He wrote, "There is nothing out there or if there is, we can have no knowledge of it," but avowed "I have proclaimed I believe in God" to parishioners attending his last service on Sunday. He says he does not regret writing the book, which he considered an exploration of the different ways that God might exist, and says many other clergy share his views, but are afraid to express them. (Reuter) ...*License to preach? A dime-a-dozen in the colonies. C'mon over.*

Red Whine: Can't get service people to help you? Consider Jane Fonda's advice: "If you're ever in a situation where you're not getting served or you can't get what you need, just cry," she says. Fonda, 56, says she discovered the trick in Moscow, where an elevator operator wouldn't help her until she "burst into tears", and that it worked so well that she found success with it again when she later got poor service in a restaurant. (AP) ...*Thanks, Jane, for furthering the cause of women all around the world.*

Welcome to Israel, ho-ho ha-ha hee-hee: So many tourists visiting Jerusalem become psychotic that soldiers on patrol watch for them, and a term — Jerusalem Syndrome — has been coined to refer to the problem. A 1991 study found that most commonly, the victims thought they were the Messiah (God was second, Satan third). Most of the delusional (80%) were Protestant; Catholics reported the most "mystical experiences". In one case, two men who arrived at the same time claiming to be the Messiah were put in a room together; each insisted that the other was an imposter. While most had histories of previous mental problems, 20% had no prior recorded incidents. Of one German on a multi-country tour, the doctor who lead the study said "he was sane in Egypt, sane in Greece, *meshugge* in Israel." (Washington Post) ...*Oy: keep him out of the states. He'll get a gun for sure.*

Rock-a-bye Baby: A couple having sex in the branches of a tree in a park near Windsor Castle in London got so caught up in the act that the woman lost her grasp and fell naked to the ground, breaking her leg. "The young couple had apparently gone to the Great Park for a bit of nookie," a park spokesman said. "It was a very clear case of coitus interruptus." (Reuter) ...*And stay **out** of the bell tower!*

You, You Dirty Rat: Frank Balun found that a rat which had been eating his garden plants had been caught in a squirrel trap, but was still alive. When it tried to escape, he killed it. Naturally, the Hillsdale, N.J. area Humane Society gave him two citations, charging him with "needlessly" killing the pest. The administrator of the local board of health praised Balun's actions, and promises to support him if the case goes to court. The Humane Society said the rat should have been "humanely put to sleep by injection" or "set free in a nature environment" instead of being killed by Balun. (AP) ...*Brooklyn, take note: guess what "nature environment for a rat" means in Jersey?*

If I Go, You Go, Hugo A-Go-Go: A renowned laboratory at Rockefeller University (N.Y.) has been the scene of mysterious chain of events: someone put chemicals in the coffee, set fires, and sent death threats to two female researchers. A police insider, who demanded anonymity, said the pranks took specialized knowledge, and therefore must be an inside job. "This is not the work of a janitor," the insider said. "It's the work of a mad scientist." Less anonymous police sources think the culprit is another researcher jealous of the two women's success. (AP) ...*I thought mad scientists merely tried to rule the world.*

Maybe It'll Improve Them
Rock 'n' Roll Relics Go Under the Hammer
Reuter headline

14 August 1994 . . . .

Calling Alfred Hitchcock: In a story headlined "Crash Frees 28 Million Bees", AP reported that "29 million bees" escaped after a truck accident during the morning rush hour in New York — meaning, we suppose, that they were still escaping at press time. Two beekeepers were called in for the roundup, but when they couldn't clear the roadway quickly enough, state police brought in insecticide. (AP) ...*Unit 12 here; send lots of bread and peanut butter, Code 3!*

Can't ya Take a Joke? Mark Callaghan, 35, of London was recently sentenced to 18 months in jail for mailing letters to a number of bishops and archbishops demanding payment of $845,000, else he would file false charges of sex abuse against Roman Catholic priests. Callaghan said "I would not call it blackmail," but rather it was "an exercise in imagination and pretense." He was arrested when he went to the bank to see if any deposits had been made there, as instructed in the letters. (Reuter) ...*It's not jail. Just imagine it's the pretend Hilton.*

Do, Re, who Me? By the time American students reach the eighth grade, Education Secretary Richard Riley says they should be able to "improvise a simple harmonic accompaniment to a musical melody," adding such a requirement shouldn't be too much "for a great nation." Riley said that in his own life, his first political success came in about the fifth grade, was when he was elected president of a children's music club. (AP) ...*I'd settle for eighth graders who could read, write and reason — and not think being elected club president is a "political success".*

Let us Prey: Police in Treviso, Italy, were investigating drug traffic in the area when they got tips that the best place to score coke in town was the local rectory. Apparently, Fanurio Lino Vivan, 36, the local Polish Orthodox priest, sold cocaine during parties held there. He was arrested after a search turned up a small quantity of the drug. (Reuter) ...*The higher you get, the closer you are to the Lord.*

It Pays to Advertise: When Sao Paulo (Brazil) police detectives arrested Robson Augusto do Nascimiento Araujo after a string of high-priced car thefts, they found his calling card — literally: he carried business cards showing the business name "Thefts and Holdups Ltd," with his title reading "thief". (Reuter) ...*Eh. He probably stole them.*

Loony Logic: George B. Roden is suing the state of Texas for $200 million because the state mental hospital, where he is confined, will not allow him to take karate lessons. Roden explained that he needed to learn karate "because as patients and convicts we are denied the use of guns to protect ourselves." (Reuter) ...*If you think we're gonna let you do that, you're crazy.*

Mom! I got the Job! The government-run Canada Employment Centre in Toronto sent a 17-year-old high school girl to a job opening at a local spa. She was offered the position, but unfortunately the position was on her back: they wanted her as a prostitute. Charges are expected to be filed, according to the police's "Morality Squad". (Reuter) ...*That must have been one gruelling interview.*

At Least They Kept off the Freeway: Bruce Hetrick, 36, a Delta Airlines customer service agent, and Ronald Hamilton, 32, a Delta mechanic, apparently took a quick spin around the Tuscon (Ariz.) airport. The most accessible vehicle was a 737 jetliner. A police car chased them down at the rev-up area and arrested them for theft. Hamilton was also charged with driving an aircraft under the influence. (AP) ...*Maybe they can apply at Northwest.*

Waiter! There's No Fly in My Soup: The Oregon Ridge Nature Center in Cockeysville, Md., held a seminar last weekend on the use of insects in food. Adrienne van den Beemt, a counselor at the center, said that 80 percent of the world's population eats insects. The taste? "Some say mealworms taste like creamy shrimp," she said. (AP) ...*But how many of the 80% do it on purpose?*

Is That Thing Loaded? Robbers in Dublin, Ireland, have found a new way to get carjack victims out of their vehicles quickly: they toss a live rat in through the sunroof. The victims, typically women, usually leave the door open — great for entry by the robbers, who drive off with the car and the weapon. A police spokesman said victims should stay in their cars, and "take their chances" with the rats. (Reuter) ...*It would never work in New York: the rats are too big to fit through sun roofs.*

As I Say, Not as I Do: The Rev. John K. Wibley, a fundamentalist preacher at the First Assembly of God Church (Worcester, Mass.), preached against the evils of alcohol. He told his parish he was "enticed" into a local casino last week. He said he wasn't there to gamble, but spent his time walking around, looking at the shops and restaurants. And, apparently, soaking up several free drinks: on his way home, he was arrested for drunk driving. (AP) ...*And no cavorting with hookers! Oh, never mind.*

You can Call me Ray, but *Never* **Call me Jay:** Ray and Jay Nugent of Los Angeles are fraternal twins. Ray is a contractor, but Jay seems to have had trouble with the law: he's wanted for bank robbery and attempted murder. Despite the FBI being aware that Ray has a twin brother, and that they believe Ray to be "a stable individual," Ray was recently arrested and jailed by sheriff deputies serving a warrant — for Jay. Ray is suing for $13 million: $1 million for each day he spent in jail before convincing police they got the wrong man. (AP) ...*Next time, arrest Ted.*

We Could Have Told You That
Panel: [O.J.] Media Frenzy Inevitable
AP headline

---

21 August 1994 . . . .

It Slices, It Dices: John Bobbitt, who became famous merely because his wife cut him down to size by slicing off his penis and tossing it in the street, has sent his lawyer to the divorce court in an effort to regain custody of the knife. But the judge withheld his decision until ownership of the knife could be properly determined. Meanwhile, Bobbitt has agreed to play himself in an "adult" movie, where he will apparently show the world his interesting scar. (AP) ...*Please! Ask the director to stop yelling "cut"!*

Yih Ha! To promote the Napa (Calif.) "Town and Country Fair," 25 longhorn cattle were put on display in the center of town, whereupon they immediately started eating the landscaping. Efforts to coax them toward the fairgrounds turned into a stampede, knocking down stop signs and ramming into police cars that were trying to corral them. "I think we're lucky no one got hurt," a police lieutenant said. (AP) ...*Mel Brooks did it better in "Blazing Saddles".*

New Concept in Nuts: Tracy Chalcraft of Chatham, Ont., bought some walnuts from the market. Upon cracking one open, she didn't find a nut, but a condom. Apparently, a nearby sex shop sells condoms in plastic nutshells, and someone tossed one into the supermarket's bin as a joke. (Reuter) ...*Heh heh: wait until she tries the melons!*

Should Run for Emperor: Thomas Krueger, running for a seat in the Bundestag (federal legislature), is plastering Berlin with campaign posters showing him wearing nothing but a slogan painted on his body: "An honest skin." There is no word on how his opponent, a woman, plans to respond. (UPI) ...*If you win that seat, please put a towel on it before you sit down.*

No... It Really *is* Something in My Eye: As an employee of Independence Professional Fireworks, Brian Kelly lived fireworks. He died fireworks, too: his will instructed that his body be cremated, and his ashes packed in a shell and shot into the sky. His was the grand finale shell at a convention of fireworks technicians last weekend in Pennsylvania, producing red and green stars above two silver comet tails. (AP) ...*Of course, most men want to go that way.*

Wrong Turn: Visiting from the Caribbean, marathon runner Michael Alexander went for an evening jog in the San Fernando Valley, the massive suburban housing area of Los Angeles. Unfortunately, he neglected to write down the address of his sister, who he was staying with, or her telephone number. Police found him the next morning wandering in a park, just 1.5 miles from his sister's house, still unable to figure out which house was hers. (AP) ...*Tan with a picket fence. Sure, fella. Come along quietly, now.*

Coffee, Tea, or Fresh Grass? Faced with ridicule from the tabloid press that the idea was "BAA-BARIC," British Airways announced it would stop transporting live sheep from Australia for ritual slaughter in Saudi Arabia. A British MP, who happened to be on the flight, wrote a letter of protest to the airline after others on board reacted strongly to the loading of the sheep, which delayed the flight. (AP, Reuter) ...*What do you mean they're not for dinner in first class? I protest!*

Home Alone, the TV Series: She was two years old, alone, crying, and wandering around the departure area of the King Khaled International Airport in Riyadh, Saudi Arabia. Her parents couldn't be found despite multiple announcements over the public address system. Without anything else to do, controllers inquired of departing flights: on one, a man jumped up when he realized that she was one of his six children. "You know that with such a number it's easy to lose one of them in a crowded place like an airport and forget about them," he said. (AP) ...*Thankfully, the sheep made it aboard safely.*

Next Time, Call the Auto Club: Dennis Wadsworth was driving through London when his truck ran out of fuel, so he parked and went for more. Police, finding the vehicle, issued a security alert: he had left it in front of 10 Downing Street, the Prime Minister's official residence. Wadsworth returned 90 minutes later to find the truck a heap of smoking rubble — police had blown it up as a precaution. "Against the background of IRA atrocities ...we had no option," a police spokesman said. (Reuter) ...*Oh, just a minute: here are your keys.*

Everyone Wants to be a Critic: Mark Bridger, 35, was found guilty in a British court of causing criminal damage to a piece of "art": a dead sheep in a glass tank filled with formaldehyde. He had poured a bottle of black ink into the tank and plastered a sign on the front reading "Black Sheep". Rather than start over with a fresh white sheep, the "artist" of the work spent $1500 to clean the ink-stained one to rehabilitate the "artwork," which he valued at $38,570. Bridger was released without being sentenced to a fine or jail. (Reuter) ...*Cleaning the sheep probably decreased its value — at least, I don't want it anymore!*

International Incident: The government of Chile has apologized to three of its neighbors for a painting done by an artist who received a grant from Chile's Education Ministry. Meanwhile, Chile's foreign minister called several Venezuelans "pea brains" after they burned a Chilean flag in protest. The painting depicts the 19th century Latin American war hero Simon Bolivar as a partially nude transvestite, complete with large breasts, lacy stockings, and an upraised middle finger. The grant was part of a program to promote Chilean culture. (Reuter) ...*So what's the problem? It brought attention to Chilean culture, didn't it?*

We Appreciate the Gesture
Germany To Curb Nuke Smuggling
AP headline

28 August 1994 . . . .

The Lord Giveth, the Feds Taketh Away: When William H.
Irvin III received a government check for $836,939.19 in
June, 1992, he considered it a gift from God since he had
recently prayed for self-sufficiency. A federal court jury in
Kansas City, Mo., was unmoved: it was a computer error,
they said, not God, which boosted his $183.69 check to the
higher amount. Convicted of knowingly spending government money, filing a false tax return and money launder-
ing, he faces 43 years in prison and a $1.25 million fine. (AP)
*...Then his prayers have been answered: he won't have to buy food
or shelter for 40 years.*

Insert Tab A into Slot B as per Diagram 11 on Page 3: The
U.S. Food and Drug Administration has finally approved
the "female condom," which has been available in other
countries for a number of years, but only if it comes with
several pages of instructions with 11 diagrams showing
proper use. But what to call them to attract American
women? "We looked at names like Behold, Within, Beyond
— pretty words and pretty packages with roses or young
couples in the sunlight," said company spokeswoman
Mary Ann Leeper. Keeping modern diseases in mind, they
finally decided to take a serious approach: "Reality" comes
packaged in a plain white box. (AP) *...It'll never sell: Americans can't face reality.*

MooooOWWWWWW! Twenty-two pregnant cows worth
more than $2,000,000 were electrocuted in a freak accident
in England when lightning struck a metal pen they were
housed in. "I have heard of odd cows being struck by
lightning, but never this many in one go before," said chief
herdsman Les Timbrell. (Reuter) *...How do you think beef
jerky was invented?*

Bras to the Borscht Belt: In an organized campaign dubbed
"Knicker Aid", British women are donating their pre-diet
undergarments when they lose weight to women in Russia,
where a "decent bra" can cost a month's wages. June
Macfarlane, of Darlington, a co-founder of the plan, hopes
the large-sized garments will suit Russians thanks to their

"starchy diets". (Reuter) ...*These days, that might violate laws against the transfer of advanced technology.*

Please! Keep Those Things Quiet: A woman who noticed that her breasts made strange sounds whenever she was at high altitudes finally checked into a hospital to find out why. An x-ray at a high-altitude clinic in Frisco, Colo. (altitude 9,300 feet), showed her saline breast implants had air bubbles in them, causing a "swishing sound" when at high altitudes, where the outside air pressure is lower. (Reuter) ...*If you think that's interesting, you should hear her husband's penile implant!*

Roach Hotel: When an insecticide maker ran a contest looking for the most roach-infested house in the country, Rosemary Mitchell of Tulsa, Okla., really wanted to win, and she did. The prize: a house call from a roach expert, who estimated her one-story house harbored between 60,000 and 100,000 roaches. (AP) ...*Nice house, but what's that crunching sound when I walk?*

Tired of Working for Peanuts: A circus elephant went berserk during a performance and crushed a trainer to death before breaking through a fence and running wild through the streets of Honolulu. Two police officers stopped the rampage with multiple shots from their service handguns as the 9,000-pounder attacked another man. In a show of sympathy not for the hapless trainer but for the elephant, a local animal rights organization put flowers on the street where it was shot. "This majestic animal ...fought for its freedom and it died for it," said the president of the group. (AP) ...*Lawsuits claiming emotional distress and "irrational fear of six-foot trunks" shouldn't be far behind.*

Reform School: Two 12-year-old boys from Tampa, Fla., charged as adults with raping a 9-year-old boy at gunpoint, should start classes at the local junior high school while awaiting trial, the judge in the case said. The assistant state attorney had no objection. "As long as they're well supervised, they need to be in school," he said. (AP) ...*I'm sure some of the older boys will be happy to take care of them.*

Dive Bomber: Alfred Peters, of Westfield, Massachusetts, was out for a parachute jump last year. As he was free-falling, he hit a private plane, knocking it out of the sky — the crash killed all four people aboard. Peters, who landed safely, has now filed suit against the air traffic controllers at a nearby airport, blaming them for not passing on warnings that he was in the area. (Reuter) *...And people think I exaggerate about the lawsuits I report on.*

Regular Kind of Guy: Singer John Denver faces a year in jail on a charge of drunk driving. This second offense — he was convicted of the same charge less than a year ago — came to light when he crashed his car into a tree. Denver's publicist, however, said he didn't think Denver was drunk: "John is not the kind of person who regularly empties a fifth of scotch." (AP) *...Not regularly, just once in a while, I guess he means.*

Picard and Riker Should Investigate
Alien Smuggling Business Grows
AP headline

---

4 September 1994 . . . .

Excuses, Excuses: In June, Richard Nieves, 21, called Aurora, Ill. police and reported that he had witnessed a child's kidnapping. "People say you can speak with your eyes, and hers seemed to be saying, 'Help me. Get me out of here. Do something for me,'" Nieves said at the time. A massive police hunt turned up nothing, and after flunking a lie detector test, Nieves admitted making the story up. He was sentenced last week to two years' probation and 500 hours of community service. Why did he do it? He needed an excuse for taking a day off work as a machine operator. (AP) *...What, "I have bubonic plague" stopped working?*

Excuses II: Marla Bennetts, a technical writer in San Jose, Calif., took a day off work to see President Clinton when he visited nearby Sunnyvale. She typed an excuse note for him to sign to take to her boss. "He did, but he laughed first," she said. (Humboldt State University JournAlum magazine) *...Did he fix any typos?*

If It's for Me, I'm Not In: Zach Williams, 18, was robbed in Chattanooga, Tenn. He tried to run away and was shot to death. One of the things the robbers stole: his pager. Police, upon learning about the beeper, figured "why not?" and sent it a page. When the murderers returned the cops' call, it was traced to George Morgan, 19, and his cousin Antonio Morgan, 18, who were arrested and charged with murder. (AP) ...*Bit by bit, Darwin is being proved right.*

No Kidding: John Knight of Cornwall, England, was a busy man. He used to run — literally — between his two families: he and his wife had 12 children, and he and his mistress, about a mile away, had nine more. Each woman was aware of the situation. "Was"? "Used to"? Alas, he died last week at the age of 58, apparently of natural causes. (Reuter) ...*And probably with a smile on his face.*

Mane Event: A racehorse with the appropriate name "Devil His Due" came in second at the Whitney Handicap at the Saratoga Race Course last Saturday, winning $77,000. He was entered in the race by the Internal Revenue Service, who seized him a few days earlier in a tax case. The winnings will be applied to $4.4 million in back taxes and interest owed by his owner. (AP) ...*Only 57 more races to go, boy. You can do it!*

Delicious and Nutritious: Canada's Ottawa Citizen newspaper recently printed a recipe for Chanterelle Lemon Pasta in its food section, calling for one cup of Chanterelle mushrooms. They even provided a helpful photograph so amateur mushroom hounds could find their own growing in the wild. Unfortunately, the photograph instead showed Destroying Angels, which are deadly when eaten. (Reuter) ...*The good news: health care is free in Canada. The bad news: there's a waiting list.*

Honor Among Thieves: A low-security jail in Wetherby, England, was broken into by burglars, who stole a safe containing $1165, mostly prisoners' wages. Inmates are now complaining about poor security. (Reuter) ...*Are they sure it wasn't an inside job?*

Labelled a Thief: Keith Osborne, 47, the president of the "Labologist Society," collectors of rare and antique beer bottle labels, was convicted by a British court for beefing up his $77,000 collection by stealing some of them from the British Archives. He was sentenced to 18 months in prison. (Reuter) ...*He had to give them back, but that's ok: he still has his Picasso collection.*

All Aboard: The New York City Transit Authority has ruled that women can ride the city subways topless. New York law dictates that if a man can be somewhere without a shirt, a woman gets the same right. The decision came after arrests of women testing the ordinance on the subways. A transit police spokesman said they would comply with the new rule, but "if they were violating any other rules, like sitting on a subway bench topless smoking a cigarette, then we would take action." Smoking is not allowed in the subways. (AP) *...You gotta love a city where it's news when authorities decide to abide by the law.*

Standing Room Only: The premiere of "Armstrong's last Good Night" is a complete sell-out at the Edinburgh (Scotland) Festival, according to its producers. The play features 40 actors who cross back and forth on stage in various costumes for 90 minutes without saying a word. The play was also a success in Berlin and Paris last year. (Reuter) *...I can hardly wait for the soundtrack album to be released.*

X Marks the Spot
Search For Female Gene Narrows
AP headline

---

11 September 1994 . . . .

Northern Exposure: Two Tlingit Indian 17-year-old boys convicted in state court of robbing and beating a pizza delivery man with a bat were turned over to the Kuye'di Kuiu Kwaan Tribal Court for sentencing: banishment to separate Pacific Northwest islands for 12–18 months of solitude, a traditional Indian punishment. Besides a rudimentary shelter and emergency food rations, they will be forced to live off the land. Tribal leaders hope the time will lead to a "purification" of their criminal tendencies. "It will be a lot better than going to prison and being some guy's girlfriend," said one of the boys. (AP) *...In the meantime, society is purified of their criminal tendencies.*

Flying Pussy Alert: An animal protection group in Jerusalem says since June there have been 43 reported cases of people throwing cats out of cars, apparently in an attempt to abandon them to the streets. While most were tossed from cars "at low speed," at least one ended up hitting the windshield of another vehicle. The cat survived. (Reuter) *...Fling a cat, go to prison: it's the law.*

Well, He Snores: In a survey by Amtrak where people were asked to choose a "dream travelling companion" from a list of several well-known people, Oprah Winfrey was on top at 18%. Kevin Costner was the top male, at 10%. President and Hillary Clinton each received 5% of the votes, but the Pope: just 2%. (Reuter) *...Sure: Oprah would know all the good places to eat.*

Hit Me Again: Mark Holmes admits he kidnapped a 10-year-old girl from a London-area vicarage and subjected her to a night of "indecent assault'. Upon being sentenced to nine years in prison, he complained to the judge that the sentence was too lenient. "What sort of a sentence is that? I have ruined a girl's life and you give me nine years? I am a beast, an animal," he said. (Reuter) *...I'm sure your new cell-mate will tame you, big boy.*

Legal Coo: A Houston, Tex., attorney taking depositions in a civil case objected in court to a witness bringing her 4-month-old infant with her. He said the baby "gurgled, cooed and made other sounds," interrupting the proceedings. The judge in the case refused to grant the baby banning, but the mother agreed to leave the baby in the next room during future depositions. (AP) *...I don't know what the problem is: the baby is merely acting like a lawyer.*

Really Hungry for Seafood: A woman taking entry tickets at the Seaside (Ore.) Aquarium noticed a man who had come in earlier walking back out — with Victor, a 25-lb. lobster, under his arm. She called the manager, Keith Chandler, who gave chase. "It wasn't too difficult to spot the guy: he had a lobster under his arm," Chandler said. Victor was plopped back into his tank, and the man was plopped into the clink on theft charges. Victor is estimated to be 80 to 100 years old. (AP) *...Oh, I thought it was a free sample.*

Smile! Lam Kin-ming, 56, a Hong Kong property "tycoon", was attacked while visiting Taiwan, drugged, and, while unconscious, videotaped being sexually assaulted. When he woke up, the gang showed him the tape, promising to release prints showing his "homosexual encounter" to the media unless he paid them $1 million. Upon receiving copies of the prints, he released them to the media himself to thwart the gang; its members have been convicted of attempted blackmail and jailed. (Reuter) ...*They don't call him a "tycoon" because he's stupid.*

Seemed Like a Good Idea at the Time: The Federal Aviation Administration, in an attempt to "sensitize" employees to sexual harassment, held a workshop where male employees were forced to walk a gauntlet of female employees, who grabbed their private parts and made sexual comments to them. An air traffic controller who was forced to walk complained "I don't do these things to people so I don't feel that I need to have them done to me." He says that the FAA has ignored his complaints and he has been blackballed by management, so he has filed suit — charging sexual harassment. (AP) ...*Let's teach employees not to torture people: tie that guy to a chair while I get my lighter....*

Tax Dollars at Work II: When Sharon Taxman was fired from her teaching position in favor of a black woman, the U.S. Department of Justice sued the Piscataway (N.J.) Board of Education on her behalf, claiming reverse discrimination. A federal judge agreed and awarded her $144,000. However, for the appeal, the Justice Department is backing the Board, saying the judgment was wrong, that the firing was valid "affirmative action" to keep a black teacher on staff. "Why shouldn't educational diversity be used to protect the only Jewish business teacher?" her lawyer asked in response. (Washington Post, AP) ...*Hi, we're from the government; we're here to help you.*

Regular Crime: The smugglers tried to outsmart them, but the Russian border guards got their men, and their illegal cargo. Drugs? Stolen art treasures? No: 55 tons of cod liver oil on the way to South Korea. (AP) ...*Maybe if the pirates had swallowed some, they could have run faster.*

Insult to Injury: A rare okapi (a short-necked cousin of the giraffe) in the Copenhagen zoo apparently died from the stress after a nearby open air concert (not a rock concert — Wagner). The carcass was sent to the Copenhagen University Zoological Museum for study. Now, university officials are checking into reports that students stole the animal's meat from the museum, and used it as the centerpiece at a barbecue party. (Reuter) ...*Well done: now we know why okapi are known as "rare".*

Do You Mean in a War Area, or at Home?
Anti-Aircraft Gun
Threatens Pope's Visit
Reuter headline

---

18 September 1994 . . . .

Birds do it, Bees do it. Economists? Never: The staid Brit journal "The Economist" needed to illustrate their cover story "The Trouble With Mergers," about problems resulting from recent corporate couplings. "It's quite difficult to illustrate corporate mergers," said editor-in-chief Bill Emmott. He settled on a photograph of a pair of copulating camels. Rejecting mating elephants, hippos and rhinos, he chose the camels partly because of the old joke that a camel is "a horse designed by committee." (LA Times) ...*And don't make fun, or we'll jack up interest rates.*

Animal Kingdom II: Gorillas Nico and Samba have been together in southern England for eight years, but have never gotten around to mating. Maybe they don't know how? Keepers note they like to watch TV ("They enjoy wildlife programs," a spokeswoman says), so they are showing the animals some new videotapes — porno movies of American gorillas — in hopes the couple will imitate the acts. No hairy babies yet, though. "There is no sign yet that they have cottoned on to what it is all about," the spokeswoman said. (Reuter) ...*If sex films don't make teenage boys good lovers, why expect it out of gorillas?*

Speaking of Guerrillas: A military court in Sierra Leone convicted Warrant Officer Amara Conteh for collaboration with the rebels during attacks against government troops. Three other soldiers were sentenced to terms of 16–22 years, but the civilian judge sentenced Conteh to hang for the crime. He is 77 years old. (Reuter) ...*Well, since you aren't likely to live for 16–22 more years, here's what we're gonna do....*

Why They Need to Practice: A soldier preparing for the Hanguang 11 war games in Taiwan accidentally pushed a button. It happened to be the button that launched a live Worker Bee rocket that was set up for the exercise. The soldier was not hurt, but four others were. (Reuter) ...*Hmmmmm: I wonder how this hand grenade works.*

Similar Sized Brains: In the port city of Dubai, Bahrain, illicit drugs are harder to come by than in, say, U.S. elementary schools. So the kids there have taken to smoking ants. Police arrested several youths for intoxication, and it took the work of the Dubai police forensic lab to figure out what they were high on. Small packets of ants are selling on the street for as much as $135. (AP) ...*Like, you know, who tried this first, man?*

More Bugs: Prosecutors in Findlay, Ohio, have dropped felony wiretap charges against Judy Weising. Concerned that her daughter had fallen in with a bad crowd, she installed an automatic tape recorder on the telephone line to see what her daughter was up to. Her estranged husband found the equipment and called police. The charges were dropped after pleas from all concerned: the woman, her husband, her daughter, and the judge himself. Weising said that "parental responsibilities supersede your child's rights in certain instances, especially if you feel that their safety is at stake." She had faced a $5000 fine and two years' prison. (AP) ...*As long as she wasn't smoking ants, we're no longer concerned.*

Point in Favor of Small Cars: Lance Land, a police officer on patrol in Waxhaw, N.C., was on patrol when he noticed a two-seater sports car stalled on the railroad tracks, with a train coming. In the car was Jan Elmore and her 3-year-old son, who during the entire ordeal chanted "Mommy, the train is going to smush us. The train is going to smush us" in a "singsong voice". Land ran over and pushed the car off the tracks with about one second to spare. "I've been telling people, I'm glad it wasn't a Cadillac," he said. (AP) ...*Then again, if it were a Cadillac, it probably wouldn't have stalled on the tracks.*

Eye of the Beholder: The Sisters of Charity of the Incarnate Word, an order of Roman Catholic nuns, has closed their art exhibit "Spiritual, Sensual, Sexual" while deciding where to reopen it after harsh criticism. The exhibit, which had been in a gallery in their convent, features true-color sculptures of genitalia and oil paintings, including "Initiation", a painting of an angel having intercourse on an altar. Sister Alice Holden, the gallery's director, said she decided to open the exhibit after guidance from prayer, because "sexuality is a tremendous gift from God." Others have called the exhibit "pornographic" and "sacrilegious". Donell Hill, the featured artist, notes the sisters are "so in tune with their higher selves. They know that it's right, even if it's a little scary." (AP) ...*That figures: just when the Catholics do something that might attract Americans to the Church, it gets shut down.*

Thank God That's Settled
Janet Jackson: We're Normal
AP headline

---

25 September 1994 . . . .

This Will Hurt Me More than it Will You: A gunman apparently hired to kill a woman shot at her several times in Edwards, Colo., but missed. So he tried hitting her with rocks. He was so inept that he was still at it when police arrived, and so nervous that when confronted by the responding officer, he had a heart attack and died on the spot. The woman survived, and recognized the gunman as a longtime friend of her ex-husband. (AP) ...*Some people just never learn how to relax.*

The Fur Really Flew: The radical activist group People for the Ethical Treatment of Animals recently unveiled two ads to support their cause. One pictured River Phoenix (who died of a drug overdose last year) with the caption "I Wouldn't Be Caught Dead in Fur"; the other pictured Kurt Cobain (who shot himself in the head with a shotgun in April) with the caption "You Need Fur Like You Need a Hole in Your Head". But when the families of the dead celebrities complained about the ads, they were dropped. (AP) ...*Tell you what: I'll treat animals with at least as much respect as you show to people.*

Safety First: An explosion at a Mesa, Ariz., plant that makes air bags for cars injured seven, two critically. (AP) ...*I don't understand; shouldn't they have been ok?*

Foudroyant Festivities: Clifford Teigland, 35, a mail carrier in St. Cloud, Minn., was hit by lightning as he reached out to open the back of his mail truck. It brought back memories: 14 years ago, he was hit by lightning when he reached for the door handle of a friend's car. "That just felt like sticking my fingers in a light socket," he said. "This one is like if you stuck your whole head in the socket." (AP) ...*I'm sure you're a nice guy, but stay the hell away from my car.*

Loo News: Cosby Totten, a former miner and the executive director of the Coal Employment Project, a women miners' support group, is waging a letter-writing campaign to the U.S. Department of Labor in an attempt to improve standards for underground toilets used in coal mines. It's apparently a problem: currently, "you just go around the corner somewhere and squat," said Libby Lindsay, an 18-year mine veteran. Meanwhile, Sherpas are set to take an $11,000 toilet to the top of Mt. Everest to support a 55-member British expedition. (AP, Reuter) ...*Dammit! Somebody send a Sherpa down for a big bag of dimes! And tell him to hurry!*

The Eat-all-you-can-to-save-your-life Diet: Mitchell Rupe, 41, was sentenced to die for two murders committed during a Seattle bank robbery. Washington's death penalty includes hanging, so Rupe's lawyer argued that the death penalty would be unconstitutional since hanging might decapitate him — Rupe weighs 410 pounds. The assistant attorney general said the state might use lethal injection — or a shorter rope. The judge sent the case back for a new penalty phase hearing. (AP) ...*I'd really like to pay my debt to society, but in the meantime, pass me a box of Twinkies.*

And the Beeper. And the Chiming Watch. And: During a pre-trial hearing in the O.J. Simpson case, the prosecutor was addressing the judge when she was interrupted: "Is that counsel's phone?" she asked, turning to defense counsel Robert Shapiro. Judge Ito, noting that this was the second time Shapiro's cellphone had interrupted proceedings, told him "Next time, it's mine." (AP) ...*A quart of milk and a loaf of bread: ok, got it babe.*

Phone Home II: Joe Williams, 1, can't really talk yet. But that didn't keep him from pushing the redial button on his Loddon, England, family's phone, connecting him to his great-grandparents — on the Caribbean island of St. Lucia. No one noticed the phone off the hook: the 25-hour call ran up a $1,575 bill. (Reuter) ...*Next time, call collect.*

Fruit News: A TV show flew Robert Ehigh and his giant tomato to New York, but the 4.25-pound monster missed the world record by almost 3.5 pounds. Mel Ednie of Scotland fared better: he wasn't flown to New York, but his 12.25-pound onion broke the 11-pound world record. (AP, Reuter) ...*Let's get these guys together: I'm thinking hamburgers here — great, big ones.*

War Games II: We reported last week on the Hanguang 11 war games in Taiwan, where a soldier accidentally shot a rocket at four comrades. The fun continues: this week, a Learjet towing a drone warplane into position for anti-aircraft missile practice was shot down — by an anti-aircraft missile, which missed the drone. All aboard were killed. (Reuter) ...*Ok: we need some volunteers for the next test. Anyone. Anyone at all.*

Call Me Daniel: An unidentified man armed only with his bible climbed into the lion's den — literally — at the London zoo. He wasn't as fortunate as his biblical counterpart: he was mauled, and is in critical condition. (Reuter) ...*If he pulls through, it'll be a miracle!*

We'll Leave the Light On For You: A 14-year-old girl who was hired to babysit several children for three days finally gave up and asked for help because the parents hadn't returned after two weeks. "If I'd known all this beforehand, I wouldn't have taken the job," said the eighth-grader. (AP) ...*And if she knew she probably won't get paid, she **really** wouldn't have taken the job.*

Uh, Where'd he Plant it?

Surgeon Imprisoned for Patient's Death in Penis Implant

Reuter headline

---

2 October 1994 . . . .

In a Family Way: A committee established by Parliament to suggest how to make Britain more "family friendly" suggested that Britain participate in a European Union policy of guaranteeing new fathers three months of unpaid paternity leave. "Helping men to be involved with their children is one way of providing a positive sense of identity," the committee report said. On the other hand, a report released by a university researcher five days earlier showed that unemployed British men would prefer to wander the streets than stay home and take care of their children. (Reuter) ...*Well sure — what's the conflict in that then?*

Wasn't Done Yet: Derrick Shaw, unhappy with the sentence for his conviction of kidnapping and armed robbery, cursed the judge and called him the "house nigger". Philadelphia judge Ricardo C. Jackson called Shaw back before the bench and changed his 7–15 year sentence to the maximum: 42–85 years, plus a recommendation for no parole. (AP) ...*And another thing: uh, well, never mind.*

If you Can't Beat 'em, you Aren't Into S&M: Fun Radio's Paris talk show for teenagers wanting to talk about sex — ranging from how to wear a condom, to sadomasochism, to sodomy — was so popular that rival Skyrock sent transcripts of the show to the Higher Audio-Visual Council, France's airwave "watchdog", which issued warnings to Fun Radio. But within months, Skyrock started a competing show, hosted by a former pornographic movie actress. "We thought she was the right person, given her experience," Skyrock said. Asked by a caller what to do about his lover who shouted too much during sex, the actress suggested "All you can do is put her head in a pillow." (Reuter) ...*Sounds like a permanent solution.*

Making a Stink: The state of Massachusetts is drafting regulations prohibiting large-scale bakers to allow the odor of bread to be released into the atmosphere because it contains ethanol, which can break down into ozone, a component of smog. "If people have such a visceral response to this smell, they can bake their own bread," said the engineer at the state Department of Environmental Protection who drafted the regulation. (AP) ...*Can't be much more ethanol than is on the breath of Massachusetts politicians on a Saturday night.*

The Joke's on the People: Jacob Haugaard, a Danish comic running a joke campaign promising better weather and the "right of men to be impotent," was shocked to learn that he won a seat in parliament. "It was all a practical joke, honestly," he said. (Reuter) ...*Everyone laughed when I said I wanted to be a comedian. Well, they aren't laughing now!*

Much Better, Thank You: A Church of England bishop who retired last year created a storm of controversy by, among other things, expressing his doubts regarding the virgin birth of Jesus. He was replaced recently by Michael Turnbull. Now, a newspaper has revealed that Turnbull was convicted in 1968 of "an act of gross indecency with a male farmer in a public lavatory." Turnbull argues the incident makes him a better clergyman: "This regrettable incident all those years ago taught me much about human frailty and fragility, and about what is required of the ordained ministry," he said. (Reuter) ...*Some American TV preachers can get a lot of mileage out of that excuse.*

Raise my Hand if you Believe in Telekinesis: A poll of Americans aged 18–34 found only 9% believe that Social Security will have the money to provide them their retirement benefits, but 46% believe in UFOs. (AP) ...*Welcome to Earth. Did you bring any credit cards?*

Cut Left! Cut Right! A home exercise video O.J. Simpson finished just a week before his wife was killed will be released as planned, according to its producers. "I used to walk on the wild side, now I just walk," Simpson says on the tape. (AP) ...*And I'm careful not to step over this line, which is called the "death line", just inside the fence.*

Line of Duty: Clarence Notree, a Chicago gym teacher, reacted to a gunman shooting at his students by herding the stunned children out a door to safety, but was himself hit in the hand. After a hearing, the Illinois Industrial Commission awarded the 19-year veteran $13,447 in Worker's Compensation for his injury. But the Chicago Board of Education appealed the ruling, saying that saving the children's lives was not part of a physical education teacher's job. After an outcry, the Board agreed to approve the claim. (AP) ...*Now we know why there are shootings at schools: it's not in the teachers' job descriptions to care.*

Wanted to Prove Justice was Blind: A juror in a Santa Ana, Calif., murder trial went to the restroom to clean her contact lens. But she pulled a tube of nail glue out of her purse instead of lens cleaner, and ended up gluing her eye shut. "Please don't kick me off the jury," she implored the judge while being wheeled away by paramedics. She was back on post the next day. (AP) ...*She just wanted to find out how it all ended.*

Swiss Army Knifed: In a cost-cutting move, the Swiss Army has retired their carrier pigeon service, releasing 7,000 birds from active duty and another 24,000 from the reserves, which were taken care of by civilians. (Reuter) ...*No wonder we haven't been able to keep those war hero statues clean.*

Say You Love Me
Telescope, Squirrel At Odds
AP headline

---

9 October 1994 . . . .

Turn Back Before it's Too Late: The state government of Alaska is trying to get the word out: there is no free land available for settlers. A program did exist, but it ended in 1986. One family packed up everything and headed north; after getting half way, they decided to call and check. No free land, they were told. They kept going, calling again and again to see if they could get a different answer. They never did, but they made it to Alaska anyway, and are now on welfare. (AP) ...*Ok, here's your land: six feet wide, 800 feet long.*

Plain Brown Wrapper: British postal carrier Michael Hales, 38 — and, Reuter was careful to point out, a bachelor — was convicted and sentenced to a year in jail for stealing some of the mail he was supposed to deliver. Apparently, he learned to recognize the distinctive wrappers used by companies to ship sex toys — vibrators, condoms, and pornography — well enough to collect eight mail sacks full. "He has suffered a great deal of embarrassment and shame," his lawyer said. (Reuter) ...*Probably not until he got caught.*

Sex Toys II: China took a big step toward sexual freedom with a government-sponsored national "sex exposition" last week, featuring displays stocked with contraceptives, sex toys, a "masturbation pillow" and "Poodle Oil". The pillow's promotional video featured a woman in lace panties grinding against the pillow, with a spokeswoman mentioning "I've used it myself and can say it really feels great." A doctor gave up trying to explain its effect. "Perhaps men don't understand this, but it makes a woman feel very, very good," she said. A promotional poster for "Poodle Oil" exhorted "Gentlemen! Don't worry for your premature ejaculation. Poodle Oil can make you a real man!" The oil contains "fine Chinese drugs." (Reuter) ...*But is it made from real poodles?*

Poodle News II: As Cassie Hughes settled into her seat for her flight from Denver to Los Angeles, she noticed the carrier with her poodle, Fifi, was being loaded into another plane. When she complained to flight attendants, she was assured it was another dog, not hers. When Hughes demanded to be let off the plane to check, she says she was offered a drink instead. Fifi ended up in Nebraska, so Hughes has sued United Airlines for false imprisonment and intentional infliction of emotional distress. United has offered $1200 for her "lost baggage claim," but Hughes' complaint asks for $5 million. (AP) ...*Fifi would probably be better off in Nebraska.*

Big Stories: Sylvanus "Hambone" Smith III, 53, is getting married. He used to weigh 1000 pounds, but is now down to 700. For his wedding present, he's saving up for a special $3000 bed that can hold the couple's combined weight. Meanwhile, Leonard Brown is fighting his health insurance company, trying to get them to pay for a $50,000 medical program to reduce his weight, which is 920 pounds. "They don't consider it a disease," he said. "If you listen to people talk, well, it's your fault — you ate too much." (AP) ...*And you're here to tell us you didn't?*

This Won't Hurt a Bit: Paul Bint, 32, a former psychiatric patient, likes to play doctor. Enough, in fact, that he attended to patients in British hospitals and bragged to a friend that he was adept at taking out spleens. He pleaded guilty this week to nine charges of burglary, theft, obtaining property by deception and forging a prescription. (Reuter) ...*Theft? Obtaining property by deception? What, the spleens?*

He Said, She Said: Joseph Howard, 47, a Cincinnati bus driver, denies he ever touched a passenger who has accused him of sexual assault. But two of her personalities (one is "Mitch", her "bodyguard") say she consented to sex, others say they are witnesses to the attack, and his lawyer has asked the judge permission to question all 10 of her personalities in depositions in an attempt to find the truth. (AP) ...*And the judge wishes he retired last year.*

Desperate Criminals Nabbed: Railroad police for the Metro-North commuter line in New York stumbled across four men playing cards. They were arrested and charged with possession of a "gambling device" — a board they were using as a table to play poker on. The Manhattan district attorney's office has declined to prosecute. One of the men, an attorney, said he has played cards on the train for 28 years, and his poker group was once featured in an article in a Metro-North in-house publication. (AP) ...*Metro-North just wanted a piece of the action.*

Never Considered Cats: They had had enough. Large rats running through underground storm drains were frightening residents in Pentre, Wales, so two men tried to burn them out. But the flames ignited a pocket of methane, and the resulting explosion blew manhole covers into the air and broke windows. "It was a miracle no one was injured or killed," a fire brigade spokesman said. It was not determined if the rats were injured. (Reuter) ...*The rats are probably happy to be rid of the methane.*

I Do, I Really, *Really* Do: Tim Williams, 31, was rushing to his London wedding when he crashed his car and broke an arm and a leg. Refusing to stay in the hospital, he managed to arrive at the wedding registry for the ceremony. By the time he was cleaned up, explanations were made and the wedding performed, his pain killers wore off and he passed out. He was returned to the hospital for further treatment. (Reuter) ...*If the trip to the altar didn't kill him, the wedding night might.*

Officials: Elvis Is Still Dead

AP headline

16 October 1994 . . . .

Oh, That: New York's Herbert Steed, 63, said he had no job or income, and collected $176 in welfare every two weeks. But he was able to put down $27,000 cash to lease an apartment in the Trump Tower for six months, allegedly paid for out of $800,000 in stolen money. In addition to being charged with grand larceny, he has also been charged with failing to report the $800,000 as income to the welfare authority. (AP) *...I simply overlooked it. Slipped my mind. My mistake.*

Danger, Politicians Working: Apparently convinced that people don't know guns are dangerous, Fulton County, Georgia, (which includes Atlanta) has decreed that gun dealers put a warning label on guns that are for sale, informing the purchaser that guns increase the risk of death. The director of Gun Owners of America notes that if a warning is in order, so is a label listing the benefits of gun ownership. (AP) *...Well, guns do smoke when fired, and second-hand smoke kills, so....*

Suspicious Person: A woman that Minneapolis police described as looking "bizarre" — dressed in a robe and veil — was arrested and charged with "concealing one's identity in public". Apparently, Minnesota cops don't see too many Muslim women, who are required by their religion to wear "modest dress". A police spokesman noted the law had no exemption for concealment for religious reasons, but there was an exemption for entertainment purposes. (AP) *...Look out! She's got a loaded Koran!*

Rocky Mountain High: Six months after an on-the-job employee with a blood alcohol level of .32% killed himself when he crashed his car on company property, Coors Brewing Co. has decided to stop allowing employees to drink all the free beer they want at work. The policy had been in effect for over 100 years. (AP) ...*Not only that, but the company will now need less than half of the employee restrooms.*

The Few, The Proud: The U.S. Department of Defense is preparing plans to use women in combat, particularly as pilots. "Equal opportunity brings with it equal obligation," the assistant secretary of defense said. But the plan was criticized by Rep. Stephen Buyer (R., Indiana): "The question is, is America ready to see one of its daughters half-naked dragged by a rope through the streets of a foreign capital after she is shot down delivering combat troops to a fire fight?" (Reuter) ...*Excuse me, sir: are you suggesting we're ready to see that happen to our sons?*

Gone Already: Stanley S. Newberg fled persecution as a Jew and came to America. He did well: when he died at age 81, his estate was valued at $8.4 million. He was also grateful to the country that took him in: his will left $5.6 million in cash to the U.S. Government. Based on 1994 spending rates, the money will last just under two minutes. (AP) ...*And we thank you for the six wrenches and four vinyl binders from the bottom of our hearts.*

And the Streets are a Bit Safer Now: Wesley "Pop" Honeywood violated his parole by brandishing an unloaded gun at a neighbor. Since 1946, Honeywood has been convicted of five felonies; he is 94 years old. Not seeing jail as a problem, he said after sentencing "I'd rather go to jail than a nursing home." (AP) ...*Yeah: the food is probably better there.*

Make Money the Old Fashioned Way — Print It: Robert P. Schmitt, Jr. worked for the Threaded Currency Paper Project in the Office of Advanced Counterfeit Deterrence, U.S. Bureau of Engraving and Printing in Washington, D.C. He was convicted last week of stealing "test" currency from work. Investigators found $650,000 in cash in Schmitt's car, $500,000 in safe deposit boxes, and $350,000 in bank accounts. He faces 20 years in prison and up to $610,000 in fines. (AP) ...*Uh, will you take cash for that?*

Call of the Wild: As the Jersey (England) Wildlife Preservation Trust released a rare Mauritius pink pigeon hatchling into the wild, a Mauritius kestrel falcon swooped down and ate it. The rare falcon had been previously rescued from extinction by the Trust. (Reuter) ...*Yes. Well. Try, try again.*

Call of the Wild II: Last week for the first time, there was a women-only bullfight in Madrid. It was a sellout. Bullfighter Jesulin de Ubrique, 21, killed seven bulls. He was showered with bras, panties and carnations by the adoring audience. (Reuter) *...Ah, now I understand what "oh, lay!" really means.*

Scared the Horses: According to a new book, Britain's Queen Mother was on a tour of an "aristocrat's" home when he pushed open a bedroom door to show her the room. On the bed was a couple making love. "How nice. Perhaps we should not go further," she is reported to have said. (Reuter) *...She probably thought it was Charles.*

Scared the Horse's Ass: Cambridge, Mass., city councilor William Walsh checked out a new art exhibit at city hall that focused on "gender identity". He was shocked to find that gender identity included differences in genitals: he "confiscated" two dildos and a photo of a penis before the exhibit could open, and threatened to file a sexual harassment suit. When asked "is it art?", City Manager Robert Healy responded "I don't know. I'm not an art critic." (AP) *...We thought you already knew that boys were different from girls. Sorry.*

Aw, Nuts
Britain Looks into Contraceptives for Squirrels
Reuter headline

---

23 October 1994 . . . .

None of that Crap: The borough council of Raritan, N.J., unanimously passed an ordinance that bans cursing. Disorderly conduct, which now includes "noisy, rude or indecent behavior, by using profane, vulgar or indecent language, by making insulting remarks or comments to others," can bring a $500 fine and 90 days in jail. (AP) *...So now can we talk about your obscene tax rates?*

Meanwhile, Back in the Motherland: The Booker Prize, Britain's top literary award, has been awarded to "How

Late It Was, How Late". The book, according to one critic who had extra time on his hands, contains 4000 expletives. (Reuter) *...And one copy has been mailed by me to Anthony DeCicco, Mayor of Raritan, N.J. Enjoy, yer'onner.*

Darwin Wins Another Round: Robert Puelo, 32, was apparently being disorderly in a St. Louis market. When the clerk threatened to call police, Puelo grabbed a hot dog, shoved it in his mouth, and walked out without paying for it. Police found him unconscious in front of the store: paramedics removed the six-inch wiener from his throat, where it had choked him to death. (AP) *...Lunch inside, just desserts outside.*

Got the Story: Ruth Halikman, editor-in-chief of the campus newspaper at Columbia University — well known for its elite journalism school — needed a photo of the school's new fire engine. So when her photographer was ready, she pulled a fire alarm. "She really didn't understand what the consequences of pulling a [false] fire alarm were," the paper's managing editor said. So far, the consequences include being asked to resign from the paper, and possible misdemeanor charges. (AP) *...And you better double-check the sources she used for her article on college sex.*

You're on a Mission from God: Graham and Amanda Glasgow worked for the Salvation Army in Manchester, England, but were fired. They appealed to an industrial tribunal, saying they had been unfairly dismissed. The Salvation Army argued that the couple had no rights as employees since they were "answering a call from God" with their work. The tribunal agreed, ruling that a "contract with God" couldn't be binding on the Army and thus they were not unfairly dismissed. (Reuter) *...Lemmie see that signature on your paycheck.*

We're Civilians — We're Here to Help You: The secret RC4 algorithm used for encryption by RSA Data Security was posted on the Internet by hackers. Once public, it was studied by other programmers, who designed improvements, making it faster and more efficient. (Netsurfer Digest) *...Can you suggest any cost-cutting improvements in the stealth bomber?*

Hey, is Sexism a Religion? A federal judge in Denver has granted a prisoner permission to practice satanic rituals in his cell. Citing First Amendment rights of freedom of speech and religion, the judge said "We ought to give the devil his due." Robert James Howard plans to use candles, incense, a black robe, a chalice, a short wooden staff, and a gong in his rituals, "ideally between 2 a.m. and 5 a.m." (AP) *...One more 2 a.m. gonging and his cellmate might sacrifice him.*

Let me Off at the Next Station: Amtrak, the U.S.'s federally subsidized passenger rail service well known for poor adherence to schedules and lack of profitability, is tired of being the brunt of jokes by Jay Leno in his "Tonight Show" routines. So it cancelled all advertising on the NBC network. "I have reluctantly come to the conclusion that NBC can write Amtrak jokes faster than we can spend advertising dollars on your network," the rail line's president told the network when it pulled the ads. (Late Show News) *...Anyone who cannot spend tax dollars faster than NBC can write jokes is clearly incompetent.*

Big Pockets: Michael Toth, a former coal mine superintendent in Wheeling, W. Va., was convicted of stealing more than 29,000 tons of coal. Rather than carrying it home, he instead changed records of trucks leaving the yard and was paid cash by a conspirator at a coal brokerage. Toth faces 115 years in prison and $4.8 million in fines. (AP) *...Lessee: kill and rape a little girl, 20 years. Steal coal, 115 years. Yeah, that's about right.*

Naked Lunch: Gaslight Music in Melbourne had its annual Nude Day last weekend, where any customer who arrived without clothing was given a free CD and served a buffet lunch. The staff, consisting of a waiter, a waitress, and a pianist, were also nude. Fifty customers attended. (Reuter) *...Uh, don't health regulations require the staff to wear hair nets?*

Wanted to Go Out with a Bang: James Kimble, 32, apparently wanted to kill himself. Jennings, Mo. police suspect that Kimble purposely loosened his basement natural gas pipe, flooding the house with gas. The resulting explosion leveled his house and caused $2 million in property damage to 40 homes in the neighborhood. A TV reporter found a suicide note 100 yards from the blast. Yet Kimble was not killed. In critical condition, if he survives his injuries he faces possible criminal charges. "He could have easily ended up in the trees with the rest of the debris," the police chief said. (AP) ...*A dazed neighbor was found nearby, chanting "Kimble and bits. Kimble and bits."*

But Isn't that Expected?
New Yorkers Help Stab Victim
AP headline

---

30 October 1994 . . . .

Deck the Halls: Rare wallpaper from the 18th century Qing dynasty in China was recently discovered hanging on the walls behind the beds in a dormitory at Stoke College in Suffolk, eastern England, a girls' boarding school. The girls "used to inscribe their names on it for posterity," the headmaster said. The paper is expected to bring $45,000 at auction. (Reuter) ...*Well sure it would be worth a lot: many of them wrote their phone numbers on it.*

Glass Prison: Paulie Failla, 40, allegedly robbed a man at an automatic teller machine in New York, stabbing him in the process. Five witnesses saw the ATM holdup, which took place in a lobby area enclosed by glass doors. So the passersby leaned up against the doors to hold them closed, trapping Failla in the lobby area until police arrived to arrest him. (AP) ...*He huffed, he puffed, but couldn't blow the house arrest down.*

Phoney Sex: A summit of executive producers of daytime soap operas addressed their shows' depictions of sexual activity after a study showed that soaps average 6.64 sexual acts or references per episode. Anti-overpopulation group Population Communications International, which sponsored the summit, says that "teen-age viewers are, in particular, watching the soaps to develop their expectations of what their sex lives might be like," and encourages the soaps to show more responsible behavior. (AP) ...*Actually, their real concern is overpopulation of soap actors, not real humans.*

Crime Story: The residents of Moffett, Okla., are a bit confused. They have been notified that they have been awarded a $106,000 grant from President Clinton's "crime bill" to help control their crime. The only catch: they have to come up with a 25% ($26,500) matching payment. Great, except that $26,500 is 2.5 times the town's annual budget, there is no crime problem in Moffett, and they don't have a police department. (AP) ...*It's a bad idea. Someone might rob the bank if they find out there's $106,000 in it.*

And Another Thing: Kimberly Appelby was riding in her boyfriend's car in Doylestown, Pa. when the driver behind them started to honk his horn. Appelby asked him to stop by sticking her hand out the window and raising her middle finger. She was cited for disorderly conduct and fined $100. Her lawyer appealed the case, saying her right to free speech had been violated. Prosecutors have dropped all charges. (AP) ...*Maybe Doylestown can get a federal grant to help fight these terrible crimes.*

Did You Drop This? A federal grand jury in Philadelphia has indicted Joseph Saunders, 39, on 12 counts of bank robbery. After the 12th robbery, bank tellers found a wallet on the floor with Saunders' welfare identification card in it. If convicted on all counts, Saunders faces 245 years in prison and $3 million in fines. (AP) ...*Which he cannot pay because they're holding his wallet as evidence.*

Reach Out and Bother Someone: Takako Sato, 39, was apparently jealous of another woman because she had a happier life. So she called the other woman on the telephone to bother her about it — an average of fifty times per day over eight years, for a total of about 150,000 calls. The woman didn't complain about Sato's calls until she had a nervous breakdown. Sato has been arrested. (Reuter) ...*I didn't know I was bothering her: she never complained.*

New Collector's Item: The University of Kentucky has announced they will be changing their eight-year-old logo for their sports teams — a drawing of a roaring wildcat — because some people say the cat's tongue looks like a penis. The tongue will be redrawn. (UPI) ...*The school couldn't resist the pressure because they have no balls.*

Not as Tasty as Stovetop: Two Haitians, Patrick Louiseau, 26, and Florence Toussaint, 27, pleaded guilty to federal firearms charges after smuggling guns to Haiti. They purchased 20 handguns and a number of frozen turkeys. They thawed the turkeys, stuffed them with the guns, refroze them, and carried them overseas in their luggage. Convinced the scheme had worked, they were arrested after buying 90 more handguns. (AP) *...The poultry salesman turned them in: he got suspicious when they came back for more turkeys.*

Not a Dummy: When tax inspectors raided a textile sweat-shop in Buenos Aires, most of the employees ran for the exits. But one man donned a disguise — a dress — and posed as a mannequin. But the inspectors were not fooled by the man's disguise after spotting his "scruffy size-45 espadrilles". (Reuter) *...Too sexy for his shoes.*

I Can See How That Might Age You
55-Year-Old Woman Has Triplets
AP headline

Italian Woman, 57, Gives Birth to Triplets
Reuter headline

---

6 November 1994 . . . .

National Exposure: Thanks in part to a new interpretation of obscenity laws, the weekly Shukan Post is now Japan's number one magazine, thanks to its full-frontal nude photography. The laws' old interpretation prohibited the showing of pubic hair on nude models, but the new, more liberal photos are bringing readers in droves. "They've reinvented the magazines for younger readers, and hair nudes are certainly a part of this," said a spokesman from the All-Japan Magazine and Book Publishers and Editors' Association. Previously, scores of women were employed to scratch out any pubic hair showing in imported magazines. (Reuter) *...Talk about your culture differences: the number one magazine in the U.S. is TV Guide.*

Official Sanction: Brooklyn Criminal Court Judge Laura Jacobson acquitted a 300 pound woman of prostitution charges because she apparently did not have sex with her clients. The defendant's "foot-licking, spanking, domination and submission do not appear to fall within the category of sexual conduct referred to in the (prostitution) statute," the judge ruled. (AP) ...*Can you ask the bailiff to lead me away in handcuffs anyway?*

Hooker Crook II: New York police arrested Antonio Olmeda, 36, for solicitation after he agreed to pay an undercover officer $10 for sex. In the back of the van he was driving, police found 18 pipe bombs and other explosives, a flame thrower, a laser-sighted shotgun, several swords and machetes, 1,000 rounds of mostly illegal ammunition, a bulletproof vest, a canister of Mace, a gas mask and two sets of handcuffs. (AP) ...*Hey: I was on my way home from a yard sale, ok?*

True Love: Cathy Snelson, 29, was in a bar in Herne Bay, England waiting for a blind date when police raided the establishment looking for drugs. Dominic McDonnell, 35, was playing pool at the time of the raid. The two spent two hours sitting on the floor with their hands tied behind their backs during the police search, but were later released. Now Cathy and Dominic have married, though they didn't invite any of the police officers involved to the wedding. "But I suppose we should have done as they brought us together," Snelson said. (Reuter) ...*Hey: can you guys tie one up for me?*

Can You Keep a Secret? MI5, Britain's secret service, wants a few good women. To recruit more women as spies, MI5 Director General Stella Rimington, the service's first female chief, is travelling the country speaking to groups of professional women to encourage them to join the previously male-dominated profession. (Reuter) ...*But only if you promise to keep James Bond away from me.*

Thrill Ride: Lennell Jones, 30, stopped his van in Chicago for fuel. As he went to pay for the gas, Kevin Lomax, 21, stepped into the driver's seat and pointed a gun at Jones' wife, who jumped out of the van and started to scream. Jones ran back to find out what was wrong, only to see the van driving away. So he jumped onto a ladder on the back and climbed onto the roof. Other drivers looked on as the van sped away at 50–60 mph. "One guy in a car shouted, 'Does that guy know you are up there?'," Jones said. Lomax stopped at a service station several miles away — the van still needed fuel — and Jones jumped down and held him for police. (AP) *...The van needed me; my wife can take care of herself.*

Things that go Boom in the Night: A 15-year-old boy in Franklin, Pa., celebrated Halloween by throwing an egg into the works at the town's electrical substation. The resulting short in a 34,000-watt transformer sent a fireball into the air, creating a flash seen all over town. The boy turned himself in so he could get medical treatment for ringing in his ears. (AP) *...Now there's a medical insurance claim form I'd like to read.*

Stop, I'm Getting Out: A British passenger in a small plane jumped out just before it crashed into a mountainside in Ireland. The pilot was killed, but the passenger walked to a nearby farmhouse for help. (Reuter) *...I thought that only worked in cartoons.*

But He Told Me To: Ann Hazard, 29, of Edinburgh, Scotland, recently won a $32,500 settlement from a theatre that had employed a hypnotist. The performer brought Hazard on stage, hypnotized her, and told her to leave "by the quickest exit." She stepped off the stage, fell four feet, and broke her leg. (Reuter) *...They shouldn't have been surprised: they knew the woman was a Hazard.*

Someone Must be at Fault
Mayor Blames Weather For Arson
AP headline

---

13 November 1994 . . . .

A Sucker is Incorporated Every Minute: New York's Spy magazine caught several companies in a scam by calling them saying they represented President Clinton, and would they be interested in paying him to endorse their products? The all-American mystery meat company Spam fell for the gag and expressed interest, as did Ball Park Franks and Weight Watchers. (Reuter) *...Well sure, Spam: everyone knows how politicians like pork.*

Aw, Dad: In Ontario, Canada, one must be 19 to drink alcohol, 18 to work serving alcohol, and 14 to work in a commercial establishment. Now, Ontario's Consumer

Minister is fighting for a law that requires strippers in bars be at least 18 years old. The action was prompted by a man who complained when he found his 15-year-old daughter was dancing nude in a bar — and no laws were being broken. (UPI) ...*Wow, look at that cutie! Hey, wait a minute, she looks familiar.*

Emergency Rations: For two weeks running, U.N. convoys have been stopped by Bosnian Serbs who have confiscated the convoys' shipments of men's underwear. Women's and children's underwear was allowed to pass. (Reuter) ...*Next week, bring some nice colors — we're tired of white.*

Running on Empty: Police in York, England, have had their gasoline allocation cut by 10% so there is enough money left in the budget to cover pension contributions. Officers now patrol by foot or bicycle, taking their cars out only in emergencies. (Reuter) ...*Gives new meaning to "run the suspect downtown for questioning."*

American Gigolo: Police in Juneau, Alaska, acting on a tip, searched a hotel room and found the occupant had $10,000 in cash. Police suspected the money was from the sale of drugs, but the man said no, he was given the money by a Juneau woman because he was such a good lover. When asked, he told officers he could not remember her name. With no direct evidence of a crime, they let him go. "He left in a real hurry, but didn't say why," a police spokesman said. "Maybe he's afraid once the word gets out about him, all the women will be chasing him." (AP) ...*Or maybe their husbands will be.*

And No Good Views for the Blind, Either: Toledo, Ohio, Mayor Carty Finkbeiner offered a solution to complaints from residents about high noise levels in neighborhoods near the airport: move deaf people there. Reacting to outrage from the deaf community, the mayor said "I didn't say that it was a good or bad idea.... [just] that it was an interesting idea." (AP) ...*I'm not saying he's a smart mayor or a stupid mayor, just an interesting mayor.*

Just Visiting: Kenosha, Wis., Municipal Judge John Neuenschwander was a bit taken aback when a drunk driving suspect produced a "get out of jail free" card — one of 8000 printed and distributed by an unsuccessful candidate for town sheriff. "Clearly, the defendant had the impression it was legitimate and was going to play that trump card," the assistant city attorney said. Neuenschwander didn't give the man any jail time, but did fine him $1107 and suspended his driver's license for nine months. (AP) *...And you may not pass "Go", nor collect $200.*

Equal Protection: A federal appeals court has ruled that the Massachusetts Bay Transportation Authority unfairly disallowed the posting of an AIDS awareness advertisement which showed a wrapped condom under the headline "One of these will make you 1-1,000th of an inch larger." The transit authority argued they were protecting children passengers against obscenity, but the court rejected the argument, saying not only was the AIDS ad not obscene, but they pointed out that the transit authority lost their moral grounds when they previously allowed movie ads showing a woman eating a hot dog with the words "Come here often?" printed over her crotch. (AP) *...But your honor: everyone knows that men are obscene and women aren't.*

Hit the Road, Jack: French police escorted a truck ferrying 300,000 test tubes of frozen human semen when the Kremlin-Bicetre Hospital's sperm bank moved from outside town into Paris' Cochin Hospital. Thanks to the tight security and a convoy speed limit of 12 mph, the transfer went without incident, the bank's director said. (AP) *...No, no more donations: I gave at the office.*

Get a Clue: A Bangkok police officer was discovered to be an impostor after he saluted a superior with the wrong hand. The man apparently worked in uniform for two months directing traffic, pulling in a nice salary by extorting money from motorists. (Reuter) *...Saluted with the wrong hand, or the wrong finger?*

Drug Money: At least 75% of all currency in the Los Angeles area is contaminated with drugs, especially powdered cocaine, according to evidence presented in a federal court case. The case centers around a Los Angeles man who was carrying $30,060 in cash in his car — to a business meeting, he said. But police charged it was profits from drug trafficking when a police dog alerted that the bills had drugs on them. Although a search of the man and his car found no drugs, the cash was seized as evidence. But a forensic toxicologist testified that most money in the L.A. area contains traces of drugs — as much as a milligram per bill. The San Francisco Federal Appeals Court noted that this was enough for a police dog to detect, and ruled the presence of drugs on the cash was not enough evidence to connect the money with a drug crime. Charges against the businessman have been dropped, but "I won't feel I've won till I got my money in my hands," he said. (LA Times) ...*No wonder I go all numb when I spend large amounts of money.*

Back to Stomping Cars
Godzilla Over Mid-Life Crisis
AP headline

---

20 November 1994 . . . .

All Aboard: The astronauts aboard the U.S. space shuttle Atlantis were in space during the recent national election. During an on-orbit press conference, a reporter asked if the astronauts had voted: all six raised their hands that they had cast absentee ballots before their launch — including the French astronaut who was on board. Oops — "team spirit," said Jean-Francois Clervoy, when asked about his raised hand. (Reuter) ...*That's nothing when you consider all the dead people who voted this year.*

Earthly Delights: Michael Baughen, 64, is the Bishop of Chester (England). He and his wife, Myrtle, recently published their book, "Your Marriage", which distills their advice from their own 38-year marriage. But most readers seem to be skipping around: "Everyone seems to have picked up on the bits about sex. We are most amused," the Bishop said. "Our Flesh", the chapter on sex, suggests couples try varying sexual positions and make an effort to have fun: "After all, God meant us to enjoy sex. He made us the way we are and gave us the parts," the book says. (Reuter) ...*You mean, there's a reason my arms are this long?*

Cholesterol Cops: Virginia Hudgins of Norfolk, Va., has been charged with animal neglect. It seems Pinkie Starlight, her Vietnamese potbellied pig, weighs about 200 lbs., not the normal 65–100 lbs. the breed should weigh. Police department humane officer Mark Kumpf noted the pig's belly scrapes the ground when it stands, and is so fat that her brow covers her eyes. Hudgins faces a $2,500 fine and a year in jail. (AP) *...And no bacon for two years.*

Rumors Greatly Exaggerated: Britain's Queen Mother is not dead. The BBC accidentally flashed a notice of the royal's demise for 30 seconds until realizing its mistake. "For a matter of seconds, a line from a rehearsal script was carried," a BBC spokesman said. "We apologize for any distress it may have caused." (Reuter) *...I'm sure it's comforting for her to know that the BBC is rehearsing for the event.*

I'll See You After Class: The American Civil Liberties Union is looking into complaints that Pittsburgh's Hollidaysburg Area Senior High School is requiring students to shower after gym classes. "I'm kind of overweight," one recent female graduate complained. "For the government to compel you to expose your body they must have a compelling reason," an ACLU spokesman said. (AP) *...Gym: from the Greek gumnos, which means "naked". So the students shouldn't have to shower in the nude, but properly, they should exercise that way.*

Thank You for Calling: A new study released by Northwestern University suggests that one reason for the increase in multiple murders is that people are angry over the increased use of automated customer service devices by businesses such as law firms. "Companies are saving money, but at a price," one of the researchers reasoned. (Newsweek) *...If voice processing really pisses you off, press 7.*

Mind Your Grammars: Moorpark (Calif.) College English professor Michael Strumpf became so irritated by people's poor grammar that he started a hotline to provide advice. He also teaches local sheriff deputies how to write investigative cases that will stand up better in court. "Just a simple semicolon can make the difference between guilt and innocence," Strumpf said, retelling a story when it actually did. He also recently corrected a speaker at an event who had suggested a guest "may want a momento of your visit here." "We don't have a word 'momento,' " Strumpf harrumphed. "The word is 'memento.' " (AP) *...Strumpf, n., hallowed patron saint of writers —This is True Dictionary.*

How Convenient: Liam Cosgrave, 68, a Catholic priest, was found dead last week at the Incognito Club, a gay sauna club in downtown Dublin. Luckily for his eternal soul, one of the two *other* priests who also happened to be at the club at the time administered the Last Rites to the fallen, naked man. One newspaper report said the priest suffered a heart attack while watching pornographic movies. (UPI) ...*Uh, yes: all of us stand by here just in case we're needed. Yeah, that's it.*

Stop it or I'll Sue You: U.S. District Court Judge John P. Fullam has ordered that Brenda Butler Bryant stop suing people until she either hires a lawyer to represent her or finds a doctor who will certify her mental competence. The Philadelphia judge noted that her more than 700 handwritten suits contained no complete sentences and were filled with "incomprehensible rubbish," such as "Slavemaster Service, B/S Wholesale Club, Lane Bryant, Negro Services, BBB/KKK/LLL-Linda Lovelace/AAA." (AP) ...*Oh yeah? Well EMS/iDiot/,? booger-booger yamma cooties!*

Celebrity Spokesman: A two page ad in Hong Kong newspapers using Adolph Hitler to promote a TV station sparked outrage there. The ad ran the day after Remembrance Day ceremonies, and took more space than articles on the event. It suggested Hitler would have been more successful if he had been able to advertise on the station, known as ATV. "With our high station share he would have been assured of total domination," the ad said. (Reuter) ...*But we have his written permission, posted directly from South America!*

He'll Just Dig His Way Out
Former NATO Mole Given 12 Years
AP headline

---

27 November 1994 . . . .

Bombs Away: Robert B. Moore, 37, a pipeline patrol pilot from Independence, Kan., bragged to friends that he could hit main street with a roll of toilet paper from his plane, then apparently tried to prove it. "He missed Main Street," a police spokeswoman said. "He didn't have a very good map, apparently." He was charged with flying an airplane under the influence of alcohol and — of course — littering. (AP) ...*The fool: he could have wiped out the entire downtown area.*

Things that go Bump in the Night: Joyce Hartley's rabbits bothered the neighbors. Apparently, their constant "scratching, thumping and banging" during mating kept neighbors Ernest and Frances Haskins awake at night. So Hartley told a London court that she would build a shed for her rabbits. (Reuter) ...*They apparently need the privacy anyway.*

So Easy, You can Do It in Your Sleep: Michael Ricksgers, 37, was convicted last week of murder in the shooting death of his wife. He contended that he was not aware of, and thus not responsible for, his actions because he was asleep at the time, and that his sleepwalking behavior was the result of a sleep disorder. His wife had planned to leave him after Christmas. (AP) ...*Uh, then would you believe it was a burglar?*

Flush with Cash: The Ukraine's karbovanets banknotes are so worthless that a paper mill in Dnipropetrovsk recycles them into more useful items, such as rolls of toilet paper. The mill's director noted the paper is of high quality, and "only the color — blue, pink or green — gives away what it once was." (Reuter) ...*Yes, but how do they pay for it?*

Kings of the Air: The Flying Elvi, a Las Vegas group that dresses as Elvis Presley to parachute out of airplanes, last week sued The Flying Elvises — another Las Vegas group that does much the same thing — claiming trademark infringement. The Flying Elvises countered that they have exclusive rights from the Presley estate. Both groups apparently got the idea from the 1992 movie "Honeymoon in Vegas", which featured a horde of Elvis impersonators jumping out of a plane over Las Vegas. (AP) ...*Love me tender, love me sweet, push me out at 12,000 feet.*

Tell Billy Idol to Steer Clear: The city of San Jose, Calif., which historically has had a substantial population of people of Mexican heritage, recently recognized that fact by placing a statue of the Aztec god Quetzalcoatl in a city park. But Chet Gallagher, the head of the local Christian group Word in Warfare, organized a prayer vigil against the statue, saying that it was an idol which "can bring God's judgment on a city" and must be removed. "We believe bringing it into the city could bring more violence to the city," he said. (AP) ...*Apparently perpetrated by people from "Word in Warfare"?*

Unfair Advantage: Electoral judges in Kenya overturned the results of a 1992 election because, they found, Member of Parliament Musikari Kombo won his seat by placing a spell on voters. The court heard testimony of witchcraft rites where constituents were influenced to vote for him or die. Kombo denied the charges, but no appeal of the decision is allowed. (Reuter) ...*Maybe this explains Ted Kennedy's continued victories.*

I Want my PTV: Manuel Bonifacio, 37, has gone on a hunger strike until the Somerville, Mass. cable operator agrees to carry a 24-hour Portuguese channel at no charge. More than a quarter of the town's residents are of Portuguese descent, Bonifacio says. Will the cable company capitulate? "We would encourage Mr. Bonifacio to eat," a Time-Warner spokesman advised. (AP) ...*I'll bet the cable company can hold out longer than he can.*

When it Absolutely, Positively Has to Get There: The U.S. Department of Energy is investigating the Army's shipment of nearly a pound of plutonium — by the overnight carrier Federal Express. The clearly marked container was supposed to be shipped by a special truck to a disposal site, but FedEx accepted and delivered the radio-tight container despite shipping rules which don't allow air transport of radioactive substances. (AP) ...*Well? Did it get there by 10:30 or not?*

So There: Centonia Braswell, 21, says he "broke down crying" when he arrived at the jail. Greenville, N.C., Superior Court Judge W. Russell Duke, Jr. sentenced him to two days and the destruction of his sweatshirt, which read "Don't Ask Me For Shit" on it. The judge held Braswell in contempt for wearing the shirt when he came to court to serve jury duty. (AP) ...*You don't want to give it, and the judge won't take it.*

Note to the Queen: I Would Too!
Mandela Says He Would Accept British Knighthood
Reuter headline

4 December 1994 . . . .

Midas Touch: The U.K. started a national lottery last month, sparking gambling fever throughout the country, including in the royal palace. Queen Elizabeth was one of the winners of the first draw, picking up a 10-pound prize. But she had to share it with the others in the syndicate that purchased the ticket, including Prince Philip and the Queen Mother — 20 royal family members in all — for a net of about 80 cents per person. (Reuter) ...*Minus the cost of tickets, equals 2 pence each. I'm thrilled.*

Sticks and Stones: The town council of Virginia Gardens, Fla., has hired a private investigator to see if Sue Gage, 52, the town clerk, has been insulting people. Recent alleged affronts include "two-faced snake" and "dresses like a slut". What to do? "Definitely, she's going to be terminated," Councilman Rigoberto Diaz, who Gage allegedly called "Mr. want-to-be a policeman," said. "She should not be calling people names." She has hired a lawyer to defend her. (AP) ...*Who will, no doubt, argue that she is simply telling the truth.*

State Secrets: Japan's parliament may open up their extensive collection of pornography for public viewing. The collection includes examples of books and magazines previously declared obscene and banned from circulation. A National Diet Library spokesman said the collection could be used by social scientists studying the evolution of Japan's public morals. (Reuter) ...*It will also do more to boost library usage than any plan yet conceived.*

Crash Course: New York City police officers will be required to take new driver safety courses after being involved in more than 3300 accidents last year. Most of the accidents occurred during routine driving, not on lights-and-siren emergency calls. 1230 officers were injured in traffic accidents last year; only 20 were wounded by gunfire. (AP) *...Easy: just leave the siren on all the time.*

Boy Wonder: The town of Elland, England, is under siege: a 14-year-old boy, convicted of vandalism and theft 138 times in the past four years, is still free because English law doesn't allow the jailing of young offenders except in extraordinary circumstances. Local shopkeepers' insurance rates have soared, and some have left the town to escape the problem. "If it was up to me, I would have had him put away somewhere long ago," his father said. (Reuter) *...Isn't 138 convictions in four years extraordinary?*

Royal Visit: Two drunken 17-year-old boys from Eton school who wanted to meet the queen triggered a security alert when they climbed the wall and staggered onto the grounds of Windsor Castle. Police released them back to the school, where Prince William is expected to attend soon. (Reuter) *...In England, weirdos try to slip into the queen's bedroom for a friendly chat. In the U.S., they pepper the White House with assault rifles.*

Media Event: Cuyahoga County (Ohio) Common Pleas Judge Anthony Calabrese, Jr., sentenced Tyson Dixon, 22, to death for two murders. And, "since we have everything else on TV, let this be shown so the public can see there is swift and certain punishment," the judge ruled. Ohio has not performed an execution since 1963; 130 inmates are on its death row. (AP) *...Coming this fall! A smashing new series on the Fox Network....*

Santa Claus Wanna-be: The owner of a pawn shop in Grand Junction, Colo., came in one morning and noticed evidence of a break-in. A fire department rescue squad rescued Jimmy Lopez Santiago, who had been trapped 20 feet down the two-story building's chimney for two days. Santiago denied attempting to burglarize the store, but wouldn't say what he was doing in the chimney, which does not have an opening into the store. (AP) *...C'mon, man: I really need my sleigh back outa hock.*

Bah, Humbug: Santa Claus is not welcome in Assen, Netherlands, where Dutch traditionalists are trying to protect local customs over the white-bearded commercial corruption of their 500-year-old tradition. "We've told police to pick up anyone dressed as Santa. Holland has a real festival of its own and should support it," said Lodewijk Osse of the Assen Sinterklaas Committee. Sinterklaas arrives in Holland on December 5 by boat from Spain, and is known to either reward children for being good by leaving presents in their shoes, or punish the bad kids by taking them back to Spain in his bag. (Reuter) ...*Shopkeepers in Elland, England, are begging for a visit.*

Bogus Bagmen: Sheriff deputies in Ocala, Fla., thought they had a good thing going. They set up a fake law firm and sent letters to fugitives, saying they qualified for cash settlements from a class-action lawsuit. They intended to arrest the bad guys when they came in to collect, but when an attorney informed the sheriff that impersonation of a lawyer is a crime in Florida, the sting operation was called off. (AP) ...*It wouldn't have worked anyway: bad guys know you never get anything for free from lawyers.*

There Goes My Knighthood
Ceremonial Sword Stolen from Windsor Castle
Reuter headline

---

11 December 1994 . . . .

Malpractice: Arthur Spears, a 63-year-old London accountant, was afraid of doctors and hospitals. So much so that when he needed bladder surgery recently, he did it himself. The resulting infection killed him. "Unfortunately, (his) drastic remedy went wrong," the coroner said. "A simple operation would have solved the problem." (Reuter) ...*Oh, sure: always second-guessing the surgeon.*

Why so Irritable? The Maricopa County (Phoenix, Ariz., area) jail is just not a fun place to be anymore. To cut costs and improve safety, Sheriff Joe Arpaio banned sex magazines, smoking, and R-rated movies. The latest thing to go: coffee. "If somebody wants a daily cup of coffee, they should make sure that they don't go to jail," Arpaio said. The move should save $100,000 per year, and cut down on "hot coffee assaults". (AP) *...The next thing you know, you won't be allowed to have knives and clubs anymore.*

Case Study: Irene Wachenfeldt, 44, was teaching an adult education class at the Kristinehamn (Sweden) high school. To drive home her point to the all-woman class about the importance of loving one's body, she stripped off her clothes, saying "my body is good enough. I want you to feel the same about your bodies." At least one student was impressed: "It was one of our best lessons," Jenny Berg said. "It helped boost our self confidence." But an outcry led Wachenfeldt to resign. "Teachers are not allowed to strip during class," a school official noted. (AP) *...During recess, sure; but not during class.*

Dreaming of a White Christmas: The U.S. Circuit Court of Appeals will not allow the city of Pittsburgh to prohibit the Ku Klux Klan to erect a Christmas cross in a town square — under authority of a city-issued permit. The city said the cross's inscription, "John 3:16" violated an ordinance against displays which included "fighting words". The decision affirmed a lower court's ruling that the ordinance was unconstitutional. (AP) *...John 11:35.*

Xmas II: The Arkansas Supreme Court has ordered Jennings Osborne to tone down the Christmas display at his Little Rock home, which features more than three million lights. Neighbors complain that the spectacle brings hordes of people to look, disrupting life in their residential neighborhood. A similar battle last year led Osborne to double the size of his exhibit this year. Osborne plans an appeal to the recent ruling. (AP) *...Osborne's lawyer, no doubt, is provided by the Little Rock Electric Company.*

Drug Sniffing Dog: Suspicious customs agents in New York found five pounds of cocaine surgically implanted in a sheepdog flown as cargo from Bogota. The implant surgery caused an infection, leading the dog to not eat, so the drugs bulged from the dog's emaciated belly. Recovering nicely, customs officials are thinking of training the dog to sniff out contraband. A man who tried to claim the dog was arrested and faces 40 years in prison. (AP) *...That's five years for trying to smuggle drugs, and 35 years for what you did to the dog.*

Barnstormers: The U.K.'s Ministry of Defence recently issued a formal apology to residents of the village of Gollinglith Foot in North Yorkshire. In June, five Tornado jets practiced a bombing run on the village phone box. The run, at an altitude of only 250 feet, caused panic among farm animals; one horse died after kicking through a fence. An official admitted choosing the telephone as the target was "injudicious." (Reuter) ...*Especially considering that the fireplug is a much greater threat.*

Elementary: John Aidiniantz, 37, wanted to help fund a museum dedicated to the legendary fictional detective Sherlock Holmes. But his funding strategy didn't hold up under the magnifying glass: he has been convicted of eight counts of fraud in the scheme. (Reuter) ...*"Violence does, in truth, recoil upon the violent, and the schemer falls into the pit which he digs for another." —Sherlock Holmes*

Safe Returns: The world's largest manufacturer of condoms, London International Group Plc, reports it has reversed its financial decline and has started to make a profit again. "We're seeing growth in our core businesses," its CEO announced. (Reuter) ...*I don't even want to know where you're looking.*

Quit Looking Over Your Shoulder, Stupid
Rio Judge Outraged by Buttocks, Orders Army to End Nudism
Reuter headline

---

18 December 1994 . . . .

Jesus Wept, but it didn't make him less secure in his personhood: The Oxford University Press is considering publishing a new rewrite of the Bible that promises to be more politically correct. Among other changes, it calls Jesus "The Human One" and God "Father-Mother" to avoid sexism, and the "Right Hand" of God is now "The Mighty Hand" to avoid offending left-handers. The Archdeacon of York isn't pleased: "The traditional language of the Bible is part of its majesty. It's ludicrous to invent language in this way." (Reuter) ...*While you're at it, let's get rid of those confusing names, and number the books instead.*

Gator Aid: The Chinese alligator was on the verge of extinction in the early '80s, but an aggressive breeding campaign has brought them back in such force that scientists there are now considering birth control for the animals. Either that, China's official news agency said, or turn some of them into handbags. (Reuter) ...*Damn it, you're supposed to leave the funny lines for me.*

Treated like Cattle: Tatoos too boring? Pierced body parts too mundane? Try branding. Burning designs into skin may be the ultimate — for now — expression of individuality. Metal heated by blowtorches is "struck" on the skin for about a second. Most brands need several strikes; one woman had an intricate design of 200 strikes performed over three years. "It's not as bad as anyone would think," says New York body piercer Adam Huffman, who has brands on his arms. "It's actually kind of soothing." Each strike takes about six weeks to heal. (AP) ...*A nose ring and "Bar S" on your ass; what are you trying to tell me, dear?*

Tourist Attraction: The soil in the town of San Bernardo, Colombia, naturally mummifies many of the local dead, hence they never rot. So the corpses are being set up for display in a museum to attract tourists. Some townspeople, however, don't want their deceased relatives propped up as exhibits. "If they see that the body has mummified when it is disinterred, they ask for it to be chopped up with a machete or an axe and then burnt," one local said. (Reuter) ...*Auntie Miranda would have wanted it that way.*

Santa Clod: Playing Santa Claus at a Southampton (England) department store, Graham Webb drank red wine while attending to the kiddies. "I thought it would put color in my cheeks," he said. But when Webb stood up, he lost his balance and fell through the store's plate glass window. Padding in his costume shielded him from injury. He kept his job, but noted "my boss... told me to drink less." (Reuter) ...*I think we all understand Rudolph's red nose a little better now, too.*

Blue Flu: Eighteen of the 28 employees of the Denville (N.J.) Police Department, including 16 police officers, have won the state lottery, splitting a $27.2 million jackpot. The department's annual budget is $2 million. "Needless to say, I didn't go to work last night. I think most of us have been up all night," one patrolman said. Ellen Sandman, the township's administrator and director of public safety, noted that she was at a dinner when the news came out. "I had three people hand me their resumes because they thought there would be some openings," she said. But the police chief, one of the winners, doesn't think there will be many resignations. "Our dispatcher works two jobs and now maybe he can drop one," he said. (AP) ...*Or perhaps buy the entire town.*

Smile for the Camera: Brian Cummings, who lives on the south side of Pittsburgh, got tired of people relieving themselves in the alley near his apartment. To combat the problem, he set up a camera with a high-intensity spotlight and loudspeaker. When he spots someone on the monitor about to soil the area, the speaker screams "Please stop urinating immediately! This is a urine-free area!" while he illuminates them with the light. "The enjoyment is watching them run," he said. One woman and 16 men have been arrested in the last two months for "open lewdness". (AP) ...*Wouldn't it have been cheaper to build the poor people an outhouse?*

Learning a Trade: The U.S. Secret Service is investigating a counterfeiting ring. The gang had made a good start on $180,000 in fake $20 bills, but had not printed the backs yet, when they were discovered — in the print shop of the maximum-security Holmesburg Prison near Philadelphia. The shop, which printed materials for the city and the prison system, has been shut down until it has been determined why the operation was not discovered until an inmate tipped guards off. (AP) ...*With a little time, they could have paid reparation to their victims. But no, you had to stop this noble effort.*

Isn't that in their Job Descriptions?
Fugitives Accused of Plot
AP headline

---

25 December 1994 . . . .

Tonya, is That You? Deborah Kemp, 33, of Detroit, was
returning to her car after paying for fuel when a man
jumped into the car to steal it. Because her 6-year-old
daughter was asleep in the back of the vehicle, Kemp
wasn't about to let him get away with it. She leapt into the
passenger side, pulled her anti-theft locking bar ("The
Club") from under the seat, and started beating the carjacker with it, all while the car proceeded down the street
at up to 30 mph. Kemp eventually dragged the man out of
the moving car (which crashed) and continued to beat him.
The unidentified carjacker was hospitalized with head injuries and two broken legs; Kemp skinned her knees, and
the seat-belted child was not injured. (AP) *...Let me explain
this to you again just a little bit harder.*

Christmas Cheer I: Thelma James, the affirmative action
officer for the state of Minnesota's tax department, declared
that departmental electronic mail could not be used to send
"Merry Christmas" greetings. Rather, to keep the separation of church and state intact, greetings should say
"Happy Holidays" or "Season's Greetings" instead. The
ban was not met with universal open arms: "There are very
serious church-state issues that need to be addressed, (but)
I would not count 'Merry Christmas' greetings via e-mail
on that priority list," said Jay Tcath, executive director of
the local Jewish Community Relations Council. (AP) *...It's
nice to know that the problems in Minnesota are so much under
control that they can take time to be patronizing ...er... paternal-
istic ...uh....*

Christmas Cheer II: Kenneth Humphrey, a Henry County
(Tenn.) commissioner, high school choral director, and
local minister, and Martin Paschall, the high school band
director, apparently got into an argument over which one
would make announcements at the high school's Christmas concert. The concert was canceled after Humphrey
allegedly hit Paschall in the face with a chair during the
argument. Paschall pressed aggravated assault changes;

Humphrey was freed after posting $1000 bail. (AP) ...*I was just trying to be nice, and thought he could use a chair.*

Christmas Cheer III: One of the most popular Christmastime stage plays in the U.K. is Snow White. But between the demands of Santa's helper roles and many stagings of the play, there has been a distinct shortage of dwarf actors to play such parts this year. So at a Snow White performance in South Shields, England, children were cast in the dwarf roles. However, the director was forced to rewrite the script when two of the young actors refused to fulfill one of their roles' requirements: to kiss Snow White. "I didn't realize the prospect of giving me a peck would horrify them so much," said Snow White actress Victoria Arbiter, 20. "When they were told to kiss me, their little faces crumpled and they burst into tears." (Reuter) ...*They'll kick themselves later — hard and often.*

Pieces on Earth: The Fallbrook (Calif.) Naval Weapons Station has announced plans to dispose of an aging cache of napalm canisters, many of which are leaking the volatile mixture of gasoline, benzene and polystyrene. Environmentalists are concerned over fumes from the leaks, but the air around the site has tested cleaner than the air at a nearby high school. (Reuter) ...*Surely this isn't a surprise.*

Pieces on Earth II: For the second time in two months [6 November], someone has survived a small-plane crash by jumping out of the plane just before impact. This time, Doug Adkins survived a crash in Texas by jumping out the door. Adkins was able to go for help for the two other victims; both are alive, one is in serious condition. (AP) ...*But he didn't fall until he looked down and realized he was standing in midair.*

Party Girl: Edward Lee Gordon, 35, of Lakewood, Colo., said he was trying to be "a cool dad," and thus hired a stripper for his son's 12th birthday party. Police were called by a local photo finisher, who was tasked to develop pictures of the event. Gordon, his girlfriend Yvonne Burdette, 32, who arranged the event, and Chelsea Rose Wunderlich, 18 — the stripper — were all arrested for investigation of "sexual assault" against the boy and two 12-year-old friends. All are free while prosecutors decide what charges to bring in the case. (AP) ...*Why can't kids do something healthy, like play war with their toy guns?*

Modern Medicine: Norwegian researchers, who apparently thought the matter needed study, have determined that leeches do not like beer or garlic. However, sour cream doesn't seem to bother them: "They liked it, sucking frantically on the wall of the container." (Reuter) ...*Simple: same fat content as hospital patients' blood.*

Oh... My... *God!!*
Man Goes Berserk in Car Saleroom, Many Volvos Hurt
Reuter headline

---

1 January 1995 . . . .

Disinterested Party: Peter Erlinder, a St. Paul, Minn., law professor charged with assault, may not choose his fiancee as his attorney, the judge in the case has ruled. The woman is also the alleged assault victim in the case, but has recanted her charge that Erlinder abused her. (AP) ...*Maybe he can hire her for his divorce later.*

Got the Message: An Oklahoma City jury outraged over Charles Scott Robinson's multiple rapes of a 3-year-old girl recommended a 30,000-year sentence, since they were not allowed to sentence him to life. The judge in the case agreed with the recommendation, and gave Robinson 5000 years for each of the six counts, to be served consecutively, not concurrently. (AP) ...*No good: with time off for good behavior, the slimeball could be out in as little as 3000–4000 years.*

Banking News: China has opened a sperm bank for yaks in Tibet. Previously, "natural" mating methods were used, but this "caused degeneration, resulting in a lower quality of the yak," the Chinese Xinhua news service said. Within six years, it is expected that 100,000–200,000 ...*er...* deposits will be stored. (Reuter) ...*It takes Communists to apply the term "low-quality degenerates" to those preferring natural mating methods.*

Banking News II: Meanwhile, China's human sperm bank in Shanghai is suffering from a severe lack of *...um...* deposits, despite men being offered incentives to cooperate. Only "a few tens" of men have come forth in the last seven years, and "the majority of those had to be persuaded at length before agreeing," said a story in an official newspaper, Youth Daily. (Reuter) *...Clearly they aren't offering those low-quality degenerates the right incentives.*

On-the-job Training: Paul Ebbs, 37, was bored with his job. Not enough to do, he said. Quit and move on? Of course not: he sued his employer, the Canadian parliament, for "wrongful hiring". He won an undisclosed settlement and has now gone into private practice. Ebbs spent three years at the parliament as one of the body's lawyers, "earning" Cdn$70,000 a year for three years to perform virtually no function. Parliament did not hire anyone to replace him. (Reuter) *...Heck, we can get someone to do that for half the cost.*

Nice Doggie: Michael Brammer is an artist with a new exhibit titled "Love" in Copenhagen. The centerpiece of his show is a group of stuffed Labrador puppies. After the "artwork" caused an uproar, he explained the dogs, which were bought from a kennel, were killed and stuffed to bring attention to the many animals mistreated in Europe. (Reuter) *...Let's not let him do an exhibit calling attention to the plight of battered wives, ok?*

Hold It: The city of West Palm Beach, Fla., asked local residents to try to flush their toilets less often over Christmas weekend to try to reduce the burden on the sewage system, which was overloaded after heavy rains. "We thought that with Christmas coming on Sunday, you're going to have a lot of people over at the house," a spokesman explained. (AP) *...Thanks for coming over. Would you mind taking this along with you?*

Fiery Vitriol: A singer with the group "Freak Shop", performing at a Newcastle, Australia, nightclub, breathed fire as part of his act. The flames reached the ceiling, setting the club on fire. Of the 55 people inside the club, 11 were hospitalized and four others were treated for smoke inhalation. The building suffered extensive damage. (AP) *...And the singer has been banned from performing "Puff, the Magic Dragon" for life.*

Bleeping Idiot: Investigating a car burglary where a pager was stolen, police detectives in Ogden, Utah, tried sending a page message to the stolen device. "We wanted to see if the ding-dong would call us back. Guess what? He did," detective Scott McGregor said. The call was traced to a nearby motel, where police arrested the 13-year-old suspect. (AP) ...*Wait: for my one phone call, I have to return this message from the FBI.*

Custody Fight: Warren Woodrow Bennett Jr. and his wife Carol Ann got a divorce. But he ended up with her breasts, so she sued to get them back. Implants, that is, that she'd had removed earlier because she thought they hurt her health. "Divorce granted to wife; breast[s] to be returned to wife," the judge ruled. (AP) ...*But your honor: they were the only parts of her that I liked!*

Do It Yourself: Two men and a woman in Russellville, Ark., built their own three-bedroom home. However, it was "built entirely of stolen construction materials and furnished with stolen furniture and appliances," the county sheriff said. "We confiscated [$50,000 worth of] stolen property that filled three pickup trucks and a 20-foot-long trailer," said the investigator in the case. (AP) ...*Dang it, Bubba, I told you we were going too far by asking them to deliver.*

The Long and Short of It: Karen Redman, 41, was convicted in an Illinois court of aggravated battery for shooting her boyfriend in the leg and belly in an attempt to shoot off his penis with a .357 magnum revolver. She was acquitted, however, of attempted murder. (UPI) ...*Hey fella, just because you have a name for it doesn't mean it's murder.*

Some People are Just *So* Sensitive
Bombing Ruins Christmas Joy
AP headline

---

8 January 1995 . . . .

Double Indemnity: Harvey Rosenthal says his Miami accountant, Donal Bunsis, is responsible for his losing $235,000 in a poor investment 12 years ago. So, three years back, Rosenthal took out a $250,000 life insurance on Bunsis, naming himself beneficiary. "It took me two years [to convince Bunsis] to get the physical," he said recently. And now? "I am praying for his death," Rosenthal says. (AP) ...*Rosenthal isn't bitter. He even gave Bunsis a Christmas present: a whole case of cigarettes.*

Made Sense at the Time: Sumner Nash, 60, and his wife were having an argument: he apparently told his wife of 30 years, Gwendolen, 58, that he would have her institutionalized if she didn't do something about her weight. Later, while he slept, Gwendolen says she shot her husband to death. But afterward, the 300-pound woman found she was unable to get out of bed, so she called police to report the shooting and to get help in getting up. (AP) ...*Prison for life, sure; but six weeks in a fat farm? No way.*

Supernatural Excuse: Sheriff deputies in McMinnville, Tenn., acting on a tip, searched the bedroom of two teenage boys for a statue of the Virgin Mary stolen from a nearby church. They found the statue, being used as the finishing touch to an occult shrine set up around a circle burned into the floor, with an altar paying homage to several serial killers. "The place gave me the creeps," said deputy Robert Searcy. "I hope I never see anything like it again." The teens admitted to the theft, but told Searcy they did not practice the occult: "They told me danced around the lighted circle, but only for exercise," he said. (AP) ...*We weren't sniffing cocaine; we just were curious what it smelled like.*

Fourth Floor, Diet Center: Nine police officers in Coventry, England, on the way to search a flat for drugs, boarded an elevator to get there. An elevator rated for a maximum of eight people. It broke down from the overload, trapping them for 45 minutes until Eddie Laidle, who lived in the building, heard their pleas for help. "I told them I would get the police," Laidle said. They replied: "We are the bloody police — get the fire brigade," Laidle said. (Reuter) ...*Well, if you're going to be rude, you can stay there.*

Leave your Alibi at the Sound of the Beep: Fort Smith, Ark., police officer James Hammond came home to an interesting message on his telephone answering machine. The machine, whose recorded greeting notes he is a police officer, was allegedly called by Gary Wayne French, 33, who left the message: "Hey, I've got your dope and the money over here. Call me," and finished with his phone number. Police called and set up a meeting, and arrested French and seven other men on felony drug charges. (AP) *...Thank you for calling Fort Smith Police. To confess to murder, press 1; to confess to robbery, press 2; to confess....*

Make an Appointment: When Raymond Cuthbert left Nolan's Pharmacy in Vernon, B.C., he told employees that he would be back in half an hour to rob them. True to his word, he came back 30 minutes later. Cuthbert and an accomplice were arrested by police who were staking out the store, waiting for him. (Reuter) *...Yet another point for Darwin.*

Wanna Bet? Hundreds of soccer fans in Toronto realized that a local sports lottery was still taking bets on soccer games that were already over. Of the 1,940 betting tickets sold, 1,690 were winners. The lottery, which realized the error too late, paid out Cdn$800,000 in winnings. (Reuter) *...Who were the 250 smart guys that bet the other way?*

Look for the Union Label: The AWU-FIMME industrial trade union of New South Wales, Australia, is trying to attract new members by offering discount coupons for "full strips" in a local dance club. The strip house, Frisky Business, denied that the offer was sexist because it applied both to male and female strippers. An AWU-FIMME spokesman said no union members had complained about the offer. (Reuter) *...Maybe they haven't seen the show yet.*

And a Coke with Lots of Ice: Oskar Keysell, 31, bit into a hamburger at a London McDonald's restaurant and spit out a gold stud ear ring — and a $1500 diamond. He showed the stud to the manager, and received a replacement hamburger. When a newspaper later went to interview the restaurant manager about the extraordinary find, the manager noted: "The customer made no mention of a diamond." (Reuter) *...Did you check the fries for the other ear ring?*

Vice Versa: A CNN/USA Today poll found that President Clinton is the most admired man in America. But the next day's Harris poll reports that Clinton is no longer the "person of the year". Their winner? "A friend or relative." (Reuter, AP) *...Well, didn't we make it clear we wanted a change?*

Let me See her Portfolio First
Virgin to Sell Cut-Price Personal Finance Services
Reuter headline

15 January 1995 . . . .

Halt in the Name of the Law: Transit police assigned to New York's subways are testing a new weapon against crime: laser-sighted service pistols. Transit Police Chief Michael O'Connor said he expected the aiming devices would reduce the number of officer-involved shootings, as suspects will know a red dot on their chest means a bullet could hit that very spot and give up instead of fight. Also, he notes, it would reduce another problem: last year, in 32 shooting incidents, 12 suspects were shot by officers, but so were seven innocent bystanders. (AP) ...*Progress: now, instead of "just a minute, I have to reload," it'll be "just a minute, I have to change my batteries."*

Halt in the Name of the Law II: Raymond Bailes, 32, of New Jersey was driving through Suffern, NY, when he spotted a patrol car on the side of a road, the officer writing a citation to another driver. Bailes stopped and turned himself in to the officer, confessing he was a drunk driver. Sure enough, Bailes failed a breathalyzer test and was charged with driving while intoxicated. When asked why he stopped, "he said he thought it was a DWI road check and he didn't want to flee," a police detective said. (AP) ...*He did prove, then, that his judgment was too impaired to drive.*

Could it have been... *Satan!?* The wife of the minister of the First Love Church in Mars, Pa., accused her husband of beating her nearly to death and leaving her beside a road to die. No, Richard Rossi said, it wasn't him, but a man who looked just like him that jumped into their car and did it. Perhaps, he added, a Satanic cult was responsible. His wife later changed her story, saying it just might have been a demon in human form that performed the evil deed. Local prosecutors, perhaps not so forgiving as Rossi's wife, have charged the minister with attempted murder. (AP) ...*But it is a nice update on "the devil made me do it."*

Dress Code: Paul Cara, a London social worker, lost his appeal to an industrial tribunal, which upheld his employer's limits on his work attire. The Hackney Social Services Department had allowed Cara to wear leggings, tights and blouses to work, but balked when he showed up in a skirt. "I feel oppressed," Cara said of the ruling. (Reuter) ...*Maybe his bra is too tight.*

Stop or be Peeled: The state of Alaska bought two mechanical gorillas as traffic flagmen to direct motorists around construction zones. The $3100 beasts, complete with fluorescent vests, hard hats and gloves, were more effective than traffic lights and cheaper than hiring humans to do the work, a state transportation department spokesman said. But the Federal Highway Administration told the state that the gorillas didn't meet federal safety standards, so they've been placed in storage. "I suppose I should declare them surplus so somebody could bid on them," the spokesman said. (AP) ...*Maybe they can be used as moose crossing attendants at the university.*

Second Wind: The Associated Press issued a special correction last week, advising editors that the "elderly" Norman Vaughan had *not* climbed 3500 *miles* to the summit of Mt. Vaughan, but rather 3500 *feet*. AP blamed the error on Vaughan's guide, who said he misspoke. (AP) ...*And those crack reporters just naturally thought he did it 5000 times.*

Lame Duck: Kansas governor Joan Finney, a Democrat, was recently replaced by Republican Bill Graves. But her cat, Jesse, refused to leave the governor's mansion when Finney moved out. Finally trapped in a cage and forcibly relocated to Finney's private residence, the animal was acting "territorial" and was said to be "fat, sassy and very vocal." (AP) ...*Now wait: are we talking about the former governor or the cat?*

"Brief" is Just an Expression: Prison inmates in San Antonio, Texas, stripped of the privilege to exercise with bar bells, have taken to ordering large law books from the prison law library, strapping them together, and hefting them to get a workout. The practice has damaged some of the books, which must be provided to the inmates on request to help them with their defenses. The prison is now considering providing only photocopies of the book sections relevant to the prisoners' cases, saying this would be cheaper than replacing the damaged books. (AP) ...*I'll bet the book publishers, being lawyers, will be happy to introduce the concept of "copyright" to the Texas Department of Criminal Justice.*

Be Right Back: Jesse Plumb told his wife he'd be away on a weekend hunting trip. After he didn't return to his Phoenix home on schedule, his worried wife called the sheriff, and search teams took two days to find him. Apparently, the hunter bagged his quarry the first day: another woman, whom he spent the weekend with. His wife has now moved out, and the sheriff's office is considering billing Plumb for the search effort: $13,000 to pay for helicopters and 40 deputies' time. (AP) ...*He was game, but she was out of season.*

But Only After the Kids are Asleep
Many Moms Still OK Spanking
AP headline

---

22 January 1995 . . . .

Cops 0, Driver 1: Police in Reading, England, arrested a man for drunk driving and put him in the back of their police car. The man then locked the police car's doors, climbed into the front seat and drove away. The arresting officers "could only watch in horror as he started up the engine and sped off into the distance," a police spokesman said. The officers gave chase in the man's van, but lost him. (Reuter) ...*With nothing else to do, the officers arrested each other for stealing the van.*

Cops 0, Driver 2: In court, Anthony Pearce, 31, of Walmley, England, denied charges that he drove his motorcycle at 178.9 mph. The speed charge was dropped when prosecutors admitted Pearce's speed may have been improperly recorded. Tests showed the motorcycle could not exceed 160 mph; Pearce admitted he might have been going that fast. The speed limit where he was caught is 70. (Reuter) ...*How in the world did they catch him? They can't even keep up with a drunk in an unfamiliar car.*

Oh Good, I thought it was Serious: Embattled air carrier USAir, which has seen more than its share of crashes recently, had another recent scare: a commuter plane, cruising at 23,000 feet, lost an engine 40 miles from its destination, Pensacola, Fla. "Other than that, there were no other complications," a USAir spokeswoman said. (AP) *...Are you kidding? Have you ever tasted USAir coffee?*

Close Enough for Who it's For: Intel's CEO Andrew Grove, heavily criticized over the recent problems with the Pentium chip, promises to do better by increasing communications with customers: "We're going to have tentacles into the PC-buying community that are going to get us closer and closer to the right answers," he said. (Business Week) *...Replace your chip, Andy, and you might get the right answer the first time.*

Butterfingers: Wanda R. Condon, a nurse at Seattle's Sacred Heart Medical Center, was handling a donated human heart when she accidentally dropped it on the floor. Thinking she had contaminated it beyond use, she threw it in the trash and falsified records to say it had been shipped to a laboratory. Her deed now exposed, she has been fined $250 and a letter of reprimand has been placed in her state license file. The surgery the heart was intended for was cancelled — apparently *before* the mishap. (AP) *...For some reason, she reminds me of my first wife.*

The Lord is My Sssssshepherd: Dewey Hale, 40, of Enigma, Ga., took his rattlesnake to church. Members of the New River Free Holiness Church take the Bible literally, his cousin Martha said, so much so that they believe they should "take up serpents" as it says in the book of Mark. He took it up out of its box, and in return it bit him. "They feel he didn't die because of the snake, but that he died because it was his time to go," she said. (AP) *...It's a miracle: the snake knew what time it was.*

Savage Breast: Customs officers at a checkpoint in southern Sweden noted "something weird" about a woman's chest: it was moving. Searching her, they found 65 baby grass snakes in her bra and six lizards loose in her blouse. The unnamed 42-year-old woman claimed she intended to start a reptile farm. She is being held on smuggling charges. (AP)

...Wearing a bra big enough for 65 snakes, and she didn't think the guys would look at her chest.

Role Model: Amanda Howard, working as a teacher's aide in Little Rock, Ark., had several of her fifth grade students take care of another student who was disrupting the class: "Everybody kick his butt," Howard told the students, according to testimony in the case. As many as 10 pupils beat on Eugene Pitts, 11, enough that he needed hospital treatment. Convicted of assault, she has been sentenced to 90 days in jail. (AP) *...It was the first time the kids did what she told them to.*

Corner the Market: Police in Sydney, Australia, have arrested a man in a fraud scheme. Apparently, the unidentified man was using a certificate of guarantee in an attempt to secure large loans. The certificate indicated the man was backed by 4,590 tonnes of platinum, which would be worth $62 billion at current prices. Only 140 tonnes of platinum are mined per year; the entire world reserve is probably significantly less than 4,590 tonnes, according to metal traders. (Reuter) *...Then can I get a mortgage for my ocean-front home in Nevada?*

Twins: A Lehman Brothers vice president pleaded guilty to criminal contempt in Manhattan Criminal Court for paying his mechanic to serve jury duty for him. The impersonation came to light when the judge asked the mechanic, "Are you Andrew Levinson?" After replying "No, I'm not," the impostor excused himself for the rest room and never came back. Levinson was sentenced to 500 hours of community service. (AP) *...Great: I had to find the one honest mechanic in town.*

1.5 Weddings and a Funeral: Kenneth Dunn died in 1991. His wife, Pat, and his mistress, Jean Cooper, are fighting in a Birmingham, England, court over which one gets to be buried beside him. Dunn had two identical houses — right down to identical kitchen appliances, wallpaper and dogs named Kim — one for each woman, spending half his time at each house. According to Pat, Dunn would joke, "If I forget who I'm with, at least I'll get the dog's name right." (Reuter) *...With luck, the judge will see there are two sides.*

Grave Robbery: A British salvage team thinks they've located the spot where 16th-century explorer Sir Francis

Drake rests, off the coast of Panama. They plan to raise him to the surface and bring him home. But the British navy thinks the body should be left well enough alone. "He had an honorable burial at sea and we wish his remains to be undisturbed," a spokesman said. "I would be very hacked off if anyone came along and nabbed my body if I'd been buried at sea," he said. (Reuter) ...*Especially if you still needed it.*

Exhibit for the Defense: Toronto's Robert Douglas, 34, denies charges of sexual assault against another man, offering as evidence a doctor's report that his penis is too small for him to commit sodomy. Meanwhile, Alastair Green, 29, is suing the British Defence Ministry, saying he was psychologically damaged 10 years ago when he was an army officer. He alleges his army comrades would drag him into a common area, strip him naked, and chain him up as a display so others could laugh at his abnormally large penis. "I felt like some kind of dog," he said. (Reuter) ...*"All men are created equal" is an ideal, not an observation.*

Bloodhounds

Sperm Sniff Their Way Home, Scientists Say

Reuter headline

---

29 January 1995 . . . .

Why they call it Dope: Truck driver Irving L. Surdam III was hauling a load of furniture to New York's Kennedy airport when he suddenly started ramming cars along the way. Upon arrival, he crashed into some trees, ran from the wreckage into a terminal, and allegedly assaulted two Delta airlines employees before leaving the building — by crashing head-first through a second story window. Hospitalized for cuts, he explained to police he was "on speed" during the melee, a Port Authority spokesman said. (AP) ...*Well, in that case, ok.*

Got Her Attention: Brandon Hampson, 23, has pleaded innocent to charges of attempted second-degree murder in an attack on his girlfriend Crystal Nicole Hutchins, 20. She told police he stabbed her multiple times with a screwdriver while saying "die!" and broke her arms with a hammer. "He tried to stab my heart, but I moved and he got higher up," she said. After playing dead by holding her breath and not reacting when kicked, she lived to tell the tale — and to apply for a license to marry Hampson. (AP) *...Mommy, tell me again about how daddy proposed?*

Don't Touch Me: Maria Rodriguez, 40, a nurse in Gary, Ind., says she's tired of seeing terminal patients and their families suffer when their lives are artificially prolonged. "I would never want my family to suffer seeing me in a vegetative state, to have them mortgage their homes and go broke paying for my care," she said. To help make sure it doesn't happen, she had the words "No Code" (medical jargon for "do not resuscitate") tattooed on her torso, "Pain and comfort only. Organ donor" just below. Her unique living will is signed with her initials. "When my name gets called, I don't want anything holding me up," she said. (AP) *...I like this lady a lot, but I hope she sticks to one-piece swimsuits from now on.*

Sign Language: Three children being driven on a highway near Salem, Ore. by an adult flashed a sign at other cars that read "Help, I've been kidnapped." A concerned motorist called police on a cellular phone, and seven police cars surrounded the vehicle and pulled it to the side of the road. A desperate criminal? No, the adult was the mother of the three kids, who were just playing. "And the mom knew what the kid was doing," a disgusted state police spokesman said. Mom was released after a "stern lecture." (AP) *...Mommy, how do you spell "moron"?*

Critics be Damned: Critics blasted "Blasted", a London stage play featuring rape, cannibalism, oral sex and eye gouging, as "utterly and entirely disgusting" with "no bounds of decency." Despite, or perhaps because of, the reviews, the play has since been sold out every night. "It's not as outrageous as I was led to believe," said one attendee. However, "if they wanted to give a serious message, they should have stopped before he ate the baby," another added. (Reuter) *...Uh, I think I'll wait for the book.*

Fetch: Friendly, a German shepherd from Antioch, Ill., brought his master a human leg, apparently found in nearby woods. Search teams tried and failed to find the rest of the body, apparently a woman who was likely murdered, nor could they get the dog to lead them to the correct spot. Now that Friendly has brought back the other leg — and a second search has turned up nothing — he has been outfitted with a radio collar to see where he goes. "Gross as it may sound, the next thing we need to find is another body part," a police spokesman said. (UPI) ...*All search teams, respond to the fire hydrant, Code 3.*

Unmasked: The poster advertising a play at the Metaphore Theatre in Lille, France, was modeled after a 16th century artist's engraving of Adam and Eve. Patrick Dessaux posed two models as in the painting, but the company that put up the posters censored them by placing black triangles — virtual fig leaves — over the models' genitals. A French court has fined the company for defacing the posters, and has ordered that the posters be replaced, sans triangles. (Reuter) ...*Maybe, someday, people will understand that the human body is, in fact, the greatest possible work of art.*

Stop, I Want Off: The takeoff of a USAir commuter plane racing 92 mph down the runway in Bridgeport, W.Va., had to aborted when passenger Earl Cleaver, 36, decided he wanted off the plane. He leapt into the cockpit and wrestled the flight crew in an attempt to grab the wheel. Cleaver, who has only one leg, was grabbed by the foot by another passenger and dragged back into the passenger compartment. Cleaver has been charged with public intoxication and resisting arrest, and federal charges are pending. (AP) ...*Can't really blame him: they were heading for Pittsburgh.*

Religious Freedom: Ron Vaughn, 15, a freshman at Mendon (Mich.) High School, has been suspended for wearing the Star of David on campus. "The principal said, 'Since you're not Jewish, you're not allowed to wear it,' " Vaughn said. "But he told me I could wear a cross if I wanted to." School administrators claim the religious symbol is sometimes used to show gang affiliation. The American Civil Liberties Union is threatening the school with a lawsuit. (AP) ...*And since you're not Jewish, you better get this sewn back on before your next gym class.*

Take it as a Compliment
Blind Man Says [Princess] Diana Prettiest Woman He Ever Saw
Reuter headline

5 February 1995 . . . .

Without Remorse: Todd Johnson was convicted of stealing a San Francisco Bay Area couple's car at gunpoint. Now, he has filed suit from prison, demanding $2,794 as compensation for the loss of his personal property that was in the car when it was recovered. Police gave the items, mostly clothing, to charity, before returning the auto to its owners. (AP) ...*Plus 30 cents each for the two bullets he fired at the victims.*

Without Remorse II: Michael Sams, serving time in a British prison for kidnapping and murder, is suing Stephanie Slater, one of his kidnap victims, for libel. In "Beyond Fear", a book about her ordeal, Slater alleges that Sams also raped her. Denying the charge, Sams says "I cannot allow this [rape] allegation to go unchallenged," and demands his day in court "to establish my innocence." (Reuter) ...*Sure he kidnaps and kills women, but don't you dare accuse him of anything bad.*

Tied Up at the Office: Mayor Aristobulo Isturiz and Governor Asdrubal Aguiar of Caracas, Venezuela, publicly disagreed with a judge's ruling that overturned the mayor's closure of two food stands. Saying the pair's comments showed "a lack of respect for judicial power," Judge Luis Oquendo ordered the two politicians detained in their offices 24 hours per day for eight days. (Reuter) ...*Now we're in trouble: two politicians with nothing better to do than get some work done.*

Sorry, Wrong Number: Levittown (Pa.) plumber Michael Lasch has been picking up other plumbers' phones, police say. Investigators say he ordered "ultra call-forwarding" for at least five of his competitors — service that would allow him to program call forwarding on their phones to switch their calls to his line. Intercepting calls for help, he was able to pick the most lucrative jobs. "He took only the better customers," one victimized competitor said. The scheme unravelled when a customer called to compliment one of the victims on the great job they did, but they hadn't received any calls that day. Bell Atlantic plans to tighten up security on such services. (AP) ...*They knew something was fishy: no one ever called to compliment them before.*

Here, Catch: San Francisco mayor Frank Jordan wants to honor someone — he just doesn't know who. During an apartment fire, frantic Nina Davis tossed her three children from her third-story window into the arms of a passerby. The mother and all of the children survived. When the call later went out for the passerby to identify himself to receive his honors, *four* men stepped forward to say they had caught the kids. (AP) ...*It's that spirit of volunteerism that makes this country great.*

Rites Lite: "St. James / the Less / Catholic / Church" reads the new four-line sign in front of the Catholic church in Highland, Ind. Confused locals have been calling the church asking, basically, "huh?" Parish pastor Francis Lazar explains that the saint the church is named for, "St. James the Less," is not to be confused with his older, larger contemporary "St. James the Greater." Lazar has no plans to replace the sign. (AP) ...*And why should he? He's probably never had so many people call.*

Inflated Controversy: WZEE radio of Madison, Wis., will continue to run a condom ad despite complaints from other advertisers. A spokeswoman for Meriter Hospital and Physicians Plus, who are boycotting the station, says it isn't that it's a condom ad, but rather "the manner in which the ad is presented" — the commercial features the sounds of a couple making love. The station's general manager argues "if that ad keeps one person from getting AIDS or prevents one unwanted pregnancy, it is worth" the loss of business. (AP) ...*It's official: doctors really don't understand "bedside manner" anymore.*

No Sense of Humor: After reading an illustrated article in The Picture, a local magazine, Richard Face, a member of the Australian parliament, got boiling mad: the article featured a restaurant in Newcastle that has nude chefs to complement their topless waitresses. (Sample: "Kylie, 22, decided to hang her hooters over the hotplate when she got fed up with being a lingerie waitress.") This just "contributes to the image of Newcastle as a sleazy city," MP Dick Face complains. The restaurant's manager says the article was simply a tongue-in-cheek publicity stunt. (Australian AP) ...*And thanks to you, Richie, it worked.*

Take Off, Eh? Carnival Air Lines flight attendant Bernadette Flanagan worked her last shift, then immediately started in her new position: as flight engineer and pilot, taking off again in the same plane that she had just landed in. "What are you doing up front? You just served me coffee!" she said one passenger told her. The airline is based in Florida. (Reuter) ...*What, never heard of cross-training?*

A Little Off the Top
Hair From Beheaded Charles I Up for Auction
Reuter headline

---

12 February 1995 . . . .

Claim Check: British frequent flyer Alak Krishnan, 43, said he lost his suitcase on an airline flight — dozens and dozens of times. Over the last two years, he collected 85,000 pounds (US$135,000) in claims. Prosecutors said Krishnan would check in two or three bags, then zip one into another and claim the zipped-up bag was lost by the airline. He has been convicted of fraud. (Reuter) ...*He could have won if he had just brought in the receipts for a few hundred replacement suitcases.*

Secret Taste Test: Patrice Stabile, a chemistry teacher at the Ida Price (San Jose, Calif.) Middle School, had told her class some time ago how deadly a certain chemical was. Recently, just as she was about to take a swig from her coffee, students yelled at her to stop: a 13-year-old student had poisoned it with the chemical while she was out of the room, they said. Stabile shrugged the incident off, but when a visiting police officer found out about it, he arrested the boy. (AP) ...*I guess she's used to it by now.*

Clothes are So Confining: Detroit police are on the lookout for a bottomless bank robber. After stuffing the loot in his pants and heading out the door, an explosive dye packet hidden in the money went off, staining his pants and marking him as the robber. Despite sub-freezing temperatures, the thief pulled off his pants and left them behind. (UPI) ...*Good idea. Now he won't be so easy to spot.*

Drove Him to It: David Guest, 33, of London, just got his driver's license. Such is normally not news, except that Guest has been trying for 17 years, and always failed the test. He took 632 driving lessons with eight instructors, crashing five cars in the process, to get to this point. "When I was told I'd passed, I bent down on my knees and thanked God," he said. "I feel like I have died and gone to heaven." (Reuter) ...*And now, on to his dream profession: downtown London cabbie.*

To the Woodshed: An unidentified Troy, Ohio, man, charged for injuring his son while paddling him, agreed to an unusual plea bargain: prosecutors would drop the charges if he would let police whack him with the same paddle. Once the deed was completed in his lawyer's office, the 8" paddle, emblazoned with the legend "Board of Education", was destroyed. (AP) ...*And the authorities in Troy deal with prostitutes ...how?*

To the Woodshed II: The Mississippi House of Representatives has adopted a bill to allow courts to order the paddling of convicted criminals in lieu of prison sentences. "I think this is a strong policy statement against crime," said Democrat Steve Holland, who pushed the bill through. Delaware was the last U.S. state to abolish floggings, in 1972. The last U.S. flogging, in Delaware, was in 1952. Other states are also thinking of bringing back corporal punishment, inspired by the caning of an American teenager in Singapore last year. (AP) ...*How many lashes for state representatives convicted of malfeasance?*

It's for a Good Cause: Disabled and nearly blind, Kelvin Woodall, 53, travelled from bar to bar in London with a cash box, asking for donations for "Camper Holidays for Disabled Scouts". He did well, collecting 143,647 pounds (US$224,100) over six years. Unfortunately, there is no such charity: he had made it up, and had spent the money on prostitutes. Convicted of obtaining cash by deception, he has been sentenced to two years in prison. (Reuter) ...*If only he was a scout, they wouldn't have had a case.*

Baker's Dozen: Toni Tenner argues that she was faithful to her husband. It was one of her *other* 12 personalities, Andrea, that committed adultery, causing the breakup of her marriage. Tenner's suit to increase her alimony payments has made it all the way to the Kentucky Supreme Court. In an earlier ruling, an appeals court judge said that allowing her to prevail would be "more in keeping with the psychobabble prevalent on television talk shows than with sound jurisprudence." Her attorney argues back that "The personality that considered herself married ... had been 100 percent faithful." (AP) ...*Fine: double the alimony, then give Toni her 1/13th share.*

Purrfect Crime: Chinatown food supplier Michael Chu turned quite a profit on the several brands of tuna he distributed to New York-area markets: he paid $4 a case, and sold 33,000 cases for $24, according to a federal indictment. But it isn't the high profit that got him: a shopper saw a can with the label torn off, and noted the label under it said "Seventh Heaven Tuna Treat Cat Food". If convicted on the nine counts of fraud he's been charged with, Chu faces 29 years in prison. (AP) ...*He'll have a hard time finding a lawyer: how many attorneys haven't eaten tuna in the last few years?*

Scales of Justice
Lawyers Weigh O.J. Witnesses
AP headline

---

19 February 1995 . . . .

Overdrawn: Karen Smith of Portland, Ore., got a call from her credit union: you're overdrawn by $346,000, they told her. Thieves had stolen her ATM card and made 724 withdrawals totalling $346,770 from 48 cash machines over a 54-hour period, making nearly a million dollars in false deposits to cover their cash withdrawals. Software that is supposed to limit ATM withdrawals was not working, so the culprits were able to get another stack of cash as fast as they could reinsert the card. "From time to time, they were considerate enough to let a real customer in," a police detective noted. Five suspects have been arrested and charged with "unauthorized use of an access device", a federal offense. Smith had written the card's PIN number on another card in her wallet. (AP) ...*No problem: she has more than enough to pay back the $346,000 from the left over portion of her recent deposit.*

Overdrawn II: Telling nearby guards he was there to fix the cash machine and that they should ignore any alarms, John Comitale, 26, allegedly removed $44,000 from the ATM at the Philadelphia International Airport and fled before the guards caught on to what he was really doing. Comitale and James Samuel, also 26, have been arrested and charged with conspiracy and bank larceny. Samuel, a former armored car company employee, gave Comitale a key to the ATM and instructions on how to get to the money, the FBI said. (AP) ...*Hi, I'm here to fix the jet. Ignore any planes going down the runway.*

Just No Fun Anymore: Starting January 1, it is illegal in California to possess bear gall bladders. Also, it is no longer permissible to trip horses for entertainment. (National Review West) ...*It's about time we brought some civility to the west.*

Hurry Up: Paul Hill, sentenced to death in a Florida state court for killing two abortion clinic employees, has demanded that his lawyer stop trying to delay his execution. Roderick Vereen, a public defender, had filed a motion to delay Hill's execution until after Hill had served his federal sentence of life in prison. (AP) ...*Is he dead? Good: now we can finally kill him.*

Color Blind: California's 1st District Court of Appeal has ruled that Alameda County Deputy District Attorney William Tingle was within his legal rights to remove a juror in an attempted murder case because she was "grossly overweight", another juror because she had braided hair (he said it was "somewhat radical"), and a third for her "braids, obesity, size, [and] manner of dress". Tingle told a newspaper that he has "never liked young, obese black women, and I think they sense that." All three of the excused jurors are black, as is Tingle and the defendant in the case. According to California law, race is not a valid reason for dismissing a juror. (AP) *...What a nice precedent to set. I'm sure your mother is proud.*

Justice of the Piece: Harris County (Texas) Criminal Court-at-Law Judge J.R. Musslewhite has an interesting court-room demeanor. He repeatedly touched the buttocks and breasts of female prosecutors in court over a two-year period, the state Commission on Judicial Conduct said. In another incident, the prosecutor in a drunk driving case asked the judge if he realized he was drinking the evidence. Musslewhite is said to have responded "Yeah, I am sure glad you lost so that I didn't have to preserve [it]." The Commission has reprimanded the judge, leaving prosecutors disappointed that he was not suspended or fired. (AP) *...I'll just assume it was something distilled, rather than the urine sample.*

Stubble Trouble: Mark Barnsley, docked in a Doncaster, England jail pending trial on assault charges, complained that his short jailhouse haircut made him look like *...well...* a convict. "If I had made a court appearance in that time it would have been very detrimental to my image," he said. A court awarded him 100 pounds in damages. (Reuter) *...He didn't want the jurors to be able to see the hole in his head, I guess.*

Case Closed: Police in Warren, Ohio, are reopening investigations into several deaths that former Trumbull County Coroner Joseph A. Sudimack Jr. had ruled as suicide. The supposed suicides include a man who was shot and run over by a bulldozer and a woman who had strangulation marks around her neck. "His job is to investigate and determine the cause of death, not the best guess or what he felt that day," said a medical examiner who was called in as a consultant. Sudimack claims that a lack of funding hampered some of his investigations. (AP) *...But apparently there was enough money to buy him a rubber stamp reading "Suicide."*

Ice Cold Bear: The Southampton University (England) Department of Child Health has issued an advisory to parents of asthmatic children to freeze their kids' teddy bears. Freezing the toys for 24 hours will kill the dust mites that can cause attacks, they say. The bears should then be washed to remove the dead mites; the treatment should be repeated weekly. "There is absolutely no point in spending a lot of money on special bedding for a child if the teddy bear is full of mites," they advised. (Reuter) ...*Daddy, where's kitty cat?*

Westerners, Too
Western Lifestyle Can Kill Asians, Study Finds
Reuter headline

---

26 February 1995 . . . .

Spies Like Us: Swedish defense forces have publicly acknowledged that they erred when they accused Russia of spying on them from submarines just off Sweden's coast. After an investigation, it was determined that the Swedes haven't been tracking Russian submarines for the last three years, but, rather, swimming minks. (Reuter) ...*Russia will forgive you if you tell their coat makers exactly where that was.*

L8RDUDE: Michigan's Office of the Secretary of State is under fire for recalling a "vanity" auto license plate the office deemed offensive. The plate reads "4 RU486", a reference to the "French" abortion-inducing drug. Critics of the action point out that other vanity plates which could be considered offensive, such as CAL-GIRL, GSPOT, HORNY, HUMP, I124Q, JUGS and NADS, have not been recalled. Then there's Theresa Watt; she's had her name on her plate for 20 years: TWATT. A state spokeswoman said that 4 RU486 was recalled under the "illegal activity or substance" portion of the license plate law, but the critics retort that neither RU486 nor abortion is illegal. (AP) ...*Nor is it illegal to be horny, to have a G-spot, or to have "nads" —yet.*

L8RDUDE II: An attorney representing Howard "Wing Ding" Jones, who had just been convicted of selling drugs, was in court in Norristown, Pa., with his client to argue that the judge should not raise Jones' bail because he was not a flight risk. Just as the judge disagreed and raised the bail from $1000 to $150,000, Jones proved the judge right: he turned and ran from the courtroom, escaping into the street. "He hit those doors like a fullback," the prosecutor noted. It took police nearly an hour to chase Jones down, at which point the judge raised Jones' bail again, to $500,000. (AP) ...*Hey, Wing Ding: maybe you can make me a special license plate....*

Minty Fresh: Carter Loar, 17, a senior at Park View High School in Sterling, Va., wanted a date. Before he asked, he pulled a small bottle of mouthwash out of his pocket and swished some through his mouth. For his gallantry, he's been suspended for 10 days and must attend a three-day substance abuse program — school rules prohibit any liquid containing alcohol on campus, and Loar's brand is about 22%. (AP) ...*I know that brand. It's great over ice with a twist.*

Pass the Pretzels: In a dispute with two local TV stations, the cable TV operator in Novato, Calif., dropped the stations out of their cable line-up. Thus, cable customer Phil Schlenker found that he could not see Monday Night Football for several weeks, and therefore had to drive to a nearby bar to watch the games. He sued the cable company and won $95 — the cost of his bar tab. When the cable company appealed the judgement, the award was reduced to $65, but the company still vows not to pay it. (Multichannel News) ...*Four bucks for a beer? Forget it!*

Winning Over an Old Flame: Last November, Mark Gallen, 45, of Benjamin River, New Brunswick, attempted suicide by pouring gasoline into the interior of his car and lighting it as he crashed the car into the living room of the house across the street from his estranged girlfriend. Failing in his suicide attempt but managing to burn the house down, he recently pleaded guilty to arson. (AP) ...*Most guys have no imagination, and would have just sent flowers.*

Snore Loser: Sari Zayed of Davis, Calif., snores. Loud enough that her next door neighbor, Chris Doherty, complained to the city, which then cited Zayed for violating the town's noise ordinance. Zayed fought the charge, which was dismissed because snoring is not a "willful act" under the law. Not satisfied with the dismissal, Zayed is suing the city for $24,500 in compensation for lost wages, medical expenses and emotional distress. (AP) ...*Fool: she could have won millions suing for "loss of sleep".*

Okies Wanna Smoke Ye: How do you one-up California's "Three Strikes and You're Out" law, which sentences criminals to life after their third felony conviction? Oklahoma proposes "Three Strikes and You're Dead" — after a third conviction, felons are sentenced to death. "People are fed up with violent crime and want something done about it," says state Rep. Bill Graves, who sponsored the bill. (AP) ...*Actually, we want something done about public servants who waste time rather than do the jobs we pay them for.*

Legislative Action II: Nevada state assemblyman Roy Neighbors has proposed naming a stretch of U.S. Highway 50 the "Extraterrestrial Alien Highway". Meanwhile, Wisconsin Rep. Tom Ourada has introduced a measure to give pilots who hit and kill deer on runways with their airplanes the right to take the carcass home to eat. (AP) ...*Doesn't USAir have enough problems without encouraging their pilots to swerve toward wildlife?*

Presidential Relations: Golfing in Bob Hope's southern California Desert Classic tournament with two other U.S. presidents, past and present, George Bush hit a ball from the rough — and into hot water. His shot hit Norma Early, 71, hard enough that it knocked her down and caused a cut on her head that needed 10 stitches. Mrs. Early apologized to Bush for getting "in the way of your shot." (AP) ...*Heck, no problem: he's had vice presidents in his way before.*

Somehow, I Just Don't See It
World Weirdness Down 2 Percent
AP headline

---

5 March 1995 . . . .

Get Better Soon: Roger Palmer, 39, who lost his right leg in an accident, applied for a special permit to park his car in spaces reserved for the handicapped. But the Hampshire County (England) Council denied the special permit, noting Palmer did not have a "permanent disability which causes inability to walk or very considerable difficulty in walking." After the denial, Palmer asked "What am I supposed to do, grow a leg?" (Reuter) ...*Another miracle brought to you by socialized medicine.*

Physician, Heal Thyself: Houston plastic surgeon Jean Cukier was having difficulty with a lamp in his office, so he decided he had better unplug it. He was rewarded with a nasty shock. Feeling lightheaded, he went into his own operating room and hooked himself up to a heart monitor, which showed an unstable rhythm. While an assistant called for an ambulance, Dr. Cukier put his defibrillator paddles on his own chest and shocked himself again, normalizing his heart beat. (USA Today) ...*My kind of doctor: cool under pressure.*

RSVP: Two hundred British soldiers who served in the Royal Signals Corps in Germany plan to attend a 10 year reunion this year. None is likely to forget to come: the invitation to the event, "Pigs Bar Reunion — 1st Saturday in June, Trafalgar Square 1995", is tattooed on their backs. A tatoo artist has been hired to append "made it" on the men who show up. (Reuter) ...*As a matter of fact, I do have an alibi for that day....*

Pro Ball: British rugby player Brendan Tuuta has been accused of assaulting an 11-year-old wheelchair-bound girl who was watching the game — and rooting for the other team. Eric Cantona, a French soccer player, has been suspended from play for the rest of the season for kicking a spectator. But British soccer player Ian Wright may be the star of the group: he was fined 5,000 pounds for giving a linesman a "V-sign", 1,500 pounds for calling a referee a "Muppet", and 750 pounds for spitting in a field security guard's face. (Reuter) ...*Pay no attention: he's just trying to set a new record.*

The Homer Simpson Diet: Studies at Chicago's Smell and Taste Treatment and Research Foundation prove the way to a man's heart is through his stomach — via his nose. No, not perfume. Doughnuts, lavender, licorice and pumpkin pie have all been shown adept at producing sexual arousal in men, according to a Foundation study. The best result so far: a combination of pumpkin pie and lavender, which increased penile blood flow in 40% of the men studied. "This suggests women have more of an effect on men if they throw away those expensive perfumes and put some pumpkin pie in the oven," one researcher suggested. (USA Today) ...*Eau de Cruller — coming soon from Chanel.*

Naturally: Princess Diana, visiting a nude beach on St. Barthelemy, noticed a nearby Frenchman, Marc Morelli, was getting ready for the sun by stripping down. "The princess began to giggle. And when she realised he was going the whole way, she burst out laughing," the Daily Mirror reported. (Reuter) ...*It wasn't until that moment that she understood Charles was lying about what "large ears" represented.*

Dress Code: It started as a dare. But Chiddix Junior High School ninth-grader Josh McElwee decided it was more an extension to a classroom lesson where students dressed in the native costumes of other nations: he came to school wearing one of his mother's floral dresses. Principal Ed Heineman didn't appreciate the learning experience, and sent McElwee home. The principal aside, "people really didn't care, except some of the seventh- and eighth-graders," McElwee said. Chiddix Junior High is located in the Illinois town of Normal. (AP) ...*Florals? In Winter? You march home right now, young man.*

Duct: It's the Cops! Police responding to a department store burglary in Orlando, Fla., cornered the suspects near large air conditioning vents. The bad guys escaped into the maze-like duct system, and could not be found. Police called off their search after 36 hours, but they aren't sure if the men got out of the building or not. "We'll wait a few days and see if we smell anything," a police spokesman said. (Reuter) ...*They'll never find them if they ended up near the snack bar.*

Service Industry: The 20,000 delegates to the U.N. World Summit for Social Development, being held this week in Copenhagen, will so stress demand for ...*uh*... local services that area call-girl establishments plan to double their escort staffing to 4,000 women. Also, local strip clubs plan to remain open 24 hours per day during the conference. "We have called in [more staff] from Thailand, eastern Europe and England," as well as Denmark, noted one strip club operator. "It's all about offering a good mix," she said.

(Reuter) *...Actually, it's all about receiving a good mix: rupees, dollars, yen, sterling....*

That Sure Helps Narrow it Down
Population Causing Problems
AP headline

---

12 March 1995 . . . .

Gimme Your Lunch Money: Stuart Possner, principal of Public School 100 in Coney Island, N.Y., has been charged with grand larceny. The indictment charges, among other crimes, that Possner sold ceramics made by kindergarten teachers with school materials and raided $11,000 in proceeds from the student candy shop. Despite a previous conviction for theft of school property in 1986, Possner has remained in his $70,000-per-year position, and was named Principal of the Year in 1992. (AP) *...Bullies need someone to look up to too.*

Stop, Look, Listen: Heliodoro Carnicero has been found guilty of negligence and fined 26,000,000 pesetas (US$200,000). It seems he herded his sheep over a train track — in front of a train travelling 60 MPH through central Spain. The train was derailed and Carnicero was seriously injured when hit by a sheep sent flying from the collision. Seventeen other people were also injured in the crash. (Reuter) *..."Tis a dainty thing to command, though 'twere but a flock of sheep." — Cervantes (Don Quixote).*

California — The Grand Canyon State: The California State Assembly had to scramble to correct a resolution last week that proclaimed Yellowstone National Park as one of the state's most treasured tourist attractions. Yellowstone is not located in California. "A typographical error," Assemblywoman Juanita McDonald claimed. Her resolution, proclaiming 1995 "State Tourism Year", passed unanimously after being corrected. (AP) *...Let's go for "State Education Year" in 1996.*

Don't Scare the Horses: Dollar Academy Headmaster John Roberston of Perth, Scotland, is tired of seeing his boarding school charges kissing and hugging in the street. Now, students of opposite sex must keep at least six inches from each other. Parents and students alike have criticized the new rule. "It is not as if we are having red-hot sex sessions in the middle of the street," said one student. (Reuter) *...Certainly not: surely they do that in private.*

Mom, He's Bugging Me: Dennis Roy Layton, 25, of Anderson, S.C., has been convicted of federal charges of electronic eavesdropping via a listening device he planted in a clock radio he had given to his 14-year-old cousin. He wanted to make sure she didn't tell her parents about their sexual affair, prosecutors said. "He always knew what we were talking about," the girl testified. Layton had explained that away by telling her that he was psychic. Layton now faces state charges of having sex with a minor. (AP) *...Tell your radio that you love me.*

Crafty Buggers II: Bangkok police raided examination rooms at the Ramkamheang army college and arrested 75 men for conspiring to cheat on the noncommissioned officers' test. The men each paid 50,000 baht (US$2,000) to get radio receivers installed in their underwear, police said, so they could listen to test answers broadcast from another room. (Reuter) *...They were easy to spot, what with the extension cords trailing out their pants' legs.*

Warning: Reading This May Be Harmful: The State of Washington wants to put warning labels on newlyweds. Not literally, but the state Senate passed a bill requiring that marriage licenses carry the disclaimer that "The laws of this state affirm your right to enter into marriage and at the same time to live within the marriage free from violence and abuse." To become law, the bill must also pass the state House of Representatives, but it has no sponsor there. (AP) *...That's because in Washington, a law doesn't apply to someone unless you pass a law saying it does.*

Bait and Snitch: Gerald Lydell Voyles, 39, was wanted for murder, and a $3,000 reward was posted for his arrest. So Voyles stopped by the jail information window in Bartow, Fla., identified himself, and tried to claim the bounty. "We believe he was serious about the reward," Sheriff Lawrence W. Crow Jr. said. "He will not be eligible." (AP) *...Damn that small print anyway.*

It Was a Typo: Jean-Charles Thomas, the bishop of Versailles, has ordered the recall of the "Bible for Christian Communities", which was written in modern, "straightforward" language. The Book, for which Thomas wrote the preface, refers to Jews as "fanatics" and their customs as "folkloric duties involving circumcision and hats". (AP) *...While you're fixing things, did you want to take a second look at "Thou shall covet thy neighbor's wife"?*

Fodor Missed This Market: Tourists have guide books for the best places to visit, but what about prisoners? Mark Leech, serving seven years in a Scottish prison for robbery, has written a guide book covering many British prisons. "It is very much a consumer's guide," Leech said. Prisoners have no say over where they spend their sentences. (Reuter) *...Which have the best soil conditions for tunnels?*

It was a Bird. No, a Plane. No, it was Chicken Little: "Meteorite impact... Does space have more in store?" demanded a panicky German newspaper. A police helicopter crew had discovered a 20-meter-wide hole blasted in the countryside outside Andechs and, after ruling out an airplane crash, declared it a meteor impact. An "expert" from Munich's city observatory fed the panic by estimating the meteor weighed 100-200 kg, and another astronomer called it "the first major comet impact in Bavaria." But no one saw it streak out of the sky. Further police inquiry found a more Earthly explanation: the man that owned the cratered land had hired a demolition expert to blast an artificial lake on his property as the centerpiece of a private wildlife refuge. "We're not quite sure who to blame for this one yet," an embarrassed police spokesman said. (Reuter) *...Have some guts: take the blame yourself.*

Naturally — Who'd Defend Him?
Man Convicted In Lawyer Murder
AP headline

---

19 March 1995 . . . .

Who? The program for the 1995 Grammy Music Awards included a special tribute to Barbra Streisand from Bill

Clinton, complete with a photograph. In case readers of the program didn't know, the White House appended a line to the bottom of the tribute: "Bill Clinton is President of the United States." (Newsweek) ...*Lest they confuse him with the guy who plays sax.*

Free Room and Board: Each March 19 for the last 218 years, hordes of swallows stop by the mission at San Juan Capistrano, Calif., in their annual 6000-mile migration. But the area around the mission has become so built up, it has become less attractive to the birds. How to encourage them to continue to nest in the area, which helps bring in thousands of tourists? Area businesses have funded an operation to seed the mission grounds with live bugs to attract the swallows, and mud pots have been set up to provide building material for nests. To make sure they get the right idea, a local artist made some clay nests, which have been placed in sight so the birds will perhaps use them for inspiration. (AP) ...*Next year, use our free shuttle!*

Nose Job: Farhad Azima, a "frequent flyer" of the supersonic Concorde airliner, paid more than $56,000 for one of the first nose cones from the plane. He plans to use the characteristic, 24-foot-long drooping cone in the back garden of his midwestern-U.S. home. (Reuter) ...*This ought to confuse the hell out of those damn gophers.*

Thank You, Please Come Again: A man in a guard uniform walked into the cashier's station at the Destin, Fla., Wal-Mart store at 3 p.m. "I'm here for the money," he said, and he was handed the day's receipts. No one suspected a thing until another guard walked in to pick up the cash; the second guard was confirmed as the real one. "They did not suspect anything unusual until another Wells Fargo guy showed up at 5 p.m.," a sheriff's spokesman said. By that time, the bogus guard had a two hour head start with his haul. (AP) ...*Check the guard route: he's probably at the next store.*

Capitalist Dog! U.S. astronaut Norm Thagard was launched on a Russian rocket to the Russian *Mir* space station this week. As part of the crew, Thagard promised to follow Russian traditions. Including the tradition, started by Yuri Gagarin, the first cosmonaut, of urinating on the tire of the bus that took the flight crew to the launch pad. (AP) ...*When in Rome, do as the Romans do.*

Tin Ear: A computer was used to play two piano pieces by Gyorgy Ligeti at the International Composers Festival in London last week because they were impossible to play by humans. "To play Ligeti's music you need five hands. This of course cuts out a number of very good performers," said Paul Patterson of the Royal Academy of Music. The computer was placed on the piano bench and wore a bow tie. (Reuter) ...*Impossible to play? Sounds more like it's impossible to listen to.*

Ja Volvo: Nason Cox, a resident of Oregon, thinks the political situation in the U.S. is going the wrong way. To illustrate his beliefs, he applied for, and received, vanity license plates for his car that read "SIG HIL" — referring to the Nazi expression "Sieg Heil". But the state has now recalled the plates, saying they are offensive. So Cox has to depend on his other car's plates to display his beliefs. They read "AK 47". (AP) ...*If the State wants your opinion, they will tell you what it is.*

Management by Wandering Around: During a radio interview, Kenneth Clarke, Britain's finance minister, noted the great success of the northern England town of Consett, saying it had "one of the best steelworks in Europe". But the steel mill was closed down 15 years ago, putting 3000 employees out of work. To redeem himself for that gaffe, last week Clarke cited another Consett factory as a major competitor in the world of disposable diapers. The town's diaper plant closed down two years ago. (Reuter) ...*Why is he giving speeches, anyway? Didn't anyone tell him he was fired six months ago?*

Family Duty: Elton and Sandra Maben of Phoenix say they couldn't control Sandra's 20-year-old son from a previous marriage, and blamed him for their eviction from their trailer. What to do? They tried to hire a hitman to kill him. The hitman, actually police detective Jack Ballentine, asked whether they had first tried more conventional methods to discipline the kid. "I tried to control him. I grabbed his lips with a pair of pliers and squeezed, but it did no good," Elton allegedly told Ballentine. Both parents have been arrested. (AP) ...*Kids these days: they just won't listen to reason.*

Hurry Up, We're on Deadline!
British Sailor Missing
AP headline at 3:06 p.m.

British Sailor Still Missing
AP headline at 3:37 p.m. the same day

26 March 1995   . . . .

The Mayor is Pleased to Announce: Washington D.C.'s Kelly Miller housing complex is a notorious hangout for drug dealers. For several months, D.C. police and federal drug agents planned out an elaborate surprise morning raid to arrest the peddlers. As 200 agents gathered for a pre-raid briefing, one of the agents said that he heard about the raid on the radio news while he was driving to the briefing. Apparently, the D.C. Department of Public and Assisted Housing, needing some good press, distributed a press release about the raid the night before. The story circulated on the regional AP newswire, and was broadcast numerous times on local radio stations starting at 9:00 p.m. the night before the raid. The surprise blown, the raid was called off. (Washington Post) ...*On the other hand, the complex probably had a nice, quiet night.*

Let No Man Put Asunder: Gary Brace, 34, apparently had a bitter divorce: he carefully divided all of his marital property in half. With a chain saw. "He wreaked havoc on the place," the prosecutor told a London court, causing 13,000 pounds in damages to the items in his ex-wife's house. The British Airways security officer was convicted of destroying property and sentenced to a year in jail. (Reuter) ...*"It was worth it," Brace murmured as he was led away....*

Neigh! In an attempt to gather more votes for their political agenda, supporters of Australia's "Daylight Saving Extension Party" staged a re-enactment of Lady Godiva's 11th century horseback protest ride. But the modern-day would-be Godiva was a victim of too much pre-event publicity. "She was going to do it naked but turned shy when she saw the media scrum," a party spokesman said

— the unnamed woman wore a g-string and t-shirt. The event was called a "bellyflop" for the Daylight Saving Party. (Australian AP) ...*Maybe she was a spy sent in by the "Keep the Voters in the Dark Party".*

Baa! Stockbrokers in Pakistan, apparently willing to try anything to turn their tumbling market around, paraded 10 black goats through the Karachi Stock Exchange and then sacrificed them in a ceremony in the building's parking lot. Trading heated up, but then prices fell even lower, after the killings. (Reuter) ...*They'd have better luck, I'm sure, if they sacrificed a few of the brokers.*

I Object: Don Bogard, facing several drug charges, pleaded guilty to one charge in hopes of getting a light sentence, but got 17.5 years. So he appealed, and was granted a full jury trial. Convicted in the trial of four felony drug charges, he was sentenced to 30 years. Last week, the 9th U.S. Circuit (San Francisco) Court of Appeals upheld the 30-year sentence. (AP) ...*If he was smart, he would have kept his mouth shut. But then again, if he was smart, he wouldn't sell PCP for a living.*

Quiet, I'm Trying to Count: Tropical termites' flatulence produces about 20% of the world's methane, a "greenhouse gas" thought to produce "global warming", says Paul Eggleton of Britain's Natural Environment Research Council. It's not the wood-eating termites people usually worry about, Eggleton says, but many of the 3000 types of soil-eating termites in tropical rain forests that are poofing out the killer gas. Eggleton's five-year project to try to find out exactly how much gas they produce estimates that the little beasties produce 80 billion kilograms of methane per year. "It's a lot of methane, but there are a lot of termites," Eggleton said. (Reuter) ...*No wonder those tropical rain forests burn so easily.*

Major Hang-Up: Jonita Anderson, 23, has been convicted of making $45,000 in "900" pay-for-service calls to psychic and horoscope hotlines, and leaving the charges unpaid on 23 different telephone lines, nine of which she used aliases to obtain. Sentenced to three years, the jail time was suspended if she can live up to one rule: "You will not make another 900 call," the judge ordered. Anderson called the hotlines for help with marital problems. "They promised to help me," she said. (AP) ...*Need help with telephone addiction? Call 1-900-Can't-Stop today!*

Is There a Script Doctor in the House? New York's Metropolitan Opera House has installed seat-back screens to show English translations of operas being staged in the house. Unfortunately, some of the charm of Italian operas may be lost when monolingists discover, for instance, that Puccini's "Madame Butterfly" includes such lyrics as "I've never sweated so much in my life" and "You mustn't cry because of those croaking frogs." (AP) ...*When you get right down to it, they're not all that much different from rock lyrics today.*

The Devil, You Say: Filita Malishipa, a Zambian woman who turned herself in to authorities for killing seven of her own children during satanic rituals, is now on trial for witchcraft. If convicted, Zambia's somewhat dated witchcraft laws mandate a fine of several cents. (Reuter) ...*Yeah, but times seven it could be as much as a quarter.*

Now We'll *Never* Hear the End of It
Scientists Identify Brain-Disabling Gene in Boys
Reuter headline

---

2 April 1995 . . . .

What am I, Chopped Beef? A 300-pound statue of the cherubic "Big Boy", the mascot of the Big Boy hamburger restaurant chain, was stolen from the front of a Toledo, Ohio, outlet and hacked to pieces by 10 boys, who are now up on charges. Various "body parts" were found around town after the ...*er*... kidnapping, each with a note attached that said "Big Boy is Dead" (except for one that said "Big Boy is almost dead. Nevermind. Now he's dead.") and signed "Pimps of pimplyness." Why? "We were bored," said Tom Martinez, 18, the Gang of 10's spokesman. He noted the stunt "was a lot of fun," but "a pretty stupid thing to do." (AP) ...*Stupid is as stupid does.*

Shark Attack: Eight men from Papua New Guinea on a five-hour boat trip ended up lost at sea for three months. Half of the crew died, but four lived through the ordeal, landing recently on Tuvalu. They survived by grabbing sharks out of the water and eating them. "We just grabbed them by the tail," one of the men said. (Reuter) ...*Turnabout is fair play.*

Space Docking Maneuver: A panel discussing extended space flight at Virginia Tech last week suggested that a private place be maintained for astronauts to socialize. "No doubt about it, if we do go to Mars, it's going to be a mixed crew," said Dwight Holland, one of the panelists. A trip to Mars and back would take several years. Former astronaut Jon McBride agreed: "It's going to be the most complicated thing we'll ever do in space flight," he said, presumably talking about the length of the mission, rather than how the crew would spend their off hours. Another panelist, who spent two years sealed in the "Biosphere II" experiment, agrees that privacy is essential. "Especially acoustical privacy," he said. (AP) ...*In space, everyone can hear you scream.*

Secret Ingredient: Hamilton, N.J., pizza delivery man Ryan Kemble, 20, delivered more than just pizza, police say. Customers using a special order code could get marijuana delivered with their pies. Undercover officers managed to buy some pot from him, they say, but they waited until he finished his deliveries before arresting him. "We know what it's like to be waiting for that pizza to come," a police spokesman said. (Reuter) ...*Your pizza delivered in 18–24 months, or it's free!*

Of Course He's Happy, He's Weird: David Weeks, a psychologist from the University of Edinburgh, has been studying eccentrics for 10 years. His conclusion: oddballs are happier than regular people. And the best part: regular people can become eccentric if they work at it. "Why should we continue to groom ourselves properly and comport ourselves according to social convention while those who flout convention seem to be having the time of their life?" Weeks asks. The best way to start on the road to oddballlality is to become unemployed — eccentrics need a lot of leisure time, he says. (AP) ...*Based on this, then, prison inmates should be ecstatic.*

Health Nut: Britain's Prince Charles has been promoting a new health drink made from herbs grown in his gardens, with proceeds going to a charity he set up. Don't like the idea of an organically grown health drink? "I'm sure you could add a drop of vodka," Charles suggests. The prince also admits that he likes to talk to plants, calling himself "potty and dotty". (Reuter) ...*I dunno what it is about him, but he seems so happy.*

On The Run: Barry Lyn Stoller, 38, wasn't satisfied with the results of his laxative, so he demanded a refund. But rather than refunding the $1.99 that Stoller paid for the product, Sandoz Corp. mailed the Seattle man a check for $98,002 — Stoller's Zip Code. According to investigators, Stoller deposited the check, then cashed out his account when it didn't bounce. He also moved out of his apartment, leaving no forwarding address. An arrest warrant charging Stoller with first degree theft has been issued. (AP) ...*Now that's innovative customer relations: issue arrest warrants when they don't like your product.*

Crown Her: Jessi Winchester is running in the "Mrs. Nevada" pageant, having won the "Mrs. Virginia City" competition. But critics complain that the 52-year-old grandmother isn't representative of Virginia City because of her profession: she's a prostitute at the Moonlight Bunny Ranch, a legal brothel. Supporters disagree: "She represents what this town and Nevada is all about. That's self-reliance, self-respect and independence," says Michael Winchester, her husband. (AP) ...*She may not win, but she's a cinch for Mrs. Congeniality.*

Don't Drink the Water: The Connecticut Food Association sponsored a reception for state lawmakers, giving them a chance to sample local food products. They made quite an impression: "I've been running back and forth to the bathroom all morning," said State Sen. Thomas Upson. Apparently, 40 of the attendees were struck with food poisoning afterward. The state health department has been asked to investigate. (AP) ...*And you can't give them antibiotics, since that instantly kills politicians.*

Now You Tell Me
Ernie Pyle Died 50 Years Ago
AP headline

9 April 1995 . . . .

Swine Flew: A South African Airways jet carrying 300 passengers from England to South Africa had to turn back and make an emergency landing. Flatulence from 72 stud pigs in its cargo hold set off a fire alarm, causing the automatic release of fire-suppressing halon gas — which suffocated 15 of the pigs. The "prize" pigs were on the passenger plane because passenger flights are "less traumatic than going on a freighter flight," an airline spokesman said. (Reuter) *...I don't think I want to know what goes on during freight flights.*

Beat It: Anath Patwardhan, a farmer in southern India, has had a long-standing problem with wild pigs damaging his crops. He used to beat drums to scare them away, but he recently found another method that is even more effective: he merely plays tapes of Michael Jackson music over loudspeakers in his fields. (Reuter) *...It's either a Jackson tape, or the sound of a jet engine.*

Hide and Seek: Albuquerque police, looking for escaped murderer Daniel Mitchem, searched his girlfriend's apartment on three separate occasions. On the third visit, the girlfriend's 2-year-old daughter pointed at the refrigerator and announced "Daddy's in there." Sure enough, he was, and apparently had eluded capture during previous searches the same way. (AP) *...Sergeant, take this man downtown and put him on ice.*

Stick'm Up Anyway: A robber burst through the door and yelled "Gimmie your money!" When his demand was met by laughter, he stopped to reconsider. "This ain't a bank anymore?" the robber asked. No, he was told, the Columbia, Tenn., bank branch had closed last summer and was now an insurance office. Undaunted, the robber took $127 from the two employees in the office. (AP) *...Not so stupid: insurance is where the really big money is.*

Yes, Master: Simpson Williams Jr., 42, was driving his Mercedes through Natchitoches, La., when, he said, the car ordered him to kill an American car. Startled, he lost control of the vehicle and struck a light pole. When a police cruiser arrived to investigate, Williams obeyed the car's command and rammed the police car — a Chevrolet. Williams has been charged with the attempted murder of the police officers in the cruiser and driving while intoxicated. (AP) *...Usually, the German cars simply compel the American cars to commit suicide.*

Ew, Gross: Researchers at the University of Sussex and London's City University are working to find out what things, in general, people find disgusting. There was a clear gender difference — "females exhibited significantly higher scores on all categories except gastroenteric products," the researchers said, pointing out that women can deal with (for instance) baby vomit better than men can, though men can better handle worms and such. (Reuter) *...And science marches onward, tirelessly searching for the ultimate: a universal disgustant.*

But They Don't Have to Look Far: The new Leicester (England) museum of health and hygiene's centerpiece is its "Flushed with Pride" exhibit, where visitors are instructed to pick up imitation feces and drop them in a transparent toilet to watch where they go. "We want to raise people's awareness of the fact that we are not living in a totally sanitized world," a museum spokesman said. (Reuter) *...Trust us: we know.*

Caught Read Handed: Warren E. Smith of Roanoke, Va., has sued Lola Rose Miller, better known as palm reader "Miss Stella", for not giving him the winning lottery numbers that she promised. The suit asks for $3 million (for the jackpot he would have won), plus $350,000 for punitive damages and actual losses of $75,724 that he paid for Miller's fees and losing lottery tickets. Miller is already serving a one-year sentence for cheating other customers. (AP) *...Smith will need time to relax at his new mountaintop ski chalet in Florida.*

Child's Play: Fined $100,000 by the Federal Communications Commission for repeated violations of a rule limiting the number of commercials that can be shown during children's programs, WSEE-TV of Erie, Pa., blamed faulty computer programming for the problem. "It was always an accident," the station's manager said. The FCC noted the violation was repeated more than 200 times. The station plans to pay the fine without an appeal. (AP) ...*The manager's five-year-old did the programming.*

Cover Up: Erena Sulkowski, a figure model for art students at Christchurch (New Zealand) Polytechnic Institute, has gone on strike. She refuses to undress for students until her pay is raised to levels paid at other art institutes, about double what she has been getting, she says. "Are we performing artists or are we just naked flesh going for cheap?" she asked. (Reuter) ...*Apparently the answer to that is evident every time you get your paycheck.*

Love Connection: Nuala Ni Chanainn, 34, in San Francisco as part of a travelling theatre group, was on a jet waiting to take off to go back home to Ireland when she decided not to go after all. She bolted off the plane at the last minute, leaving TWA airline officials thinking that she perhaps had planted a bomb on the plane and escaped. The plane and all luggage were thoroughly searched by a bomb-sniffing dog. After extensive questioning, Chanainn convinced authorities that there was no bomb: she merely couldn't bear to leave her new boyfriend. The plane was released nearly four hours later, minus the love-struck violinist, who is spending another two weeks with her beau. (AP) ...*Wait until she realizes she missed her chance to join the "mile-high club".*

Play Misty for Me: Three janitors at the Fowler Elementary School in Ceres, Calif., tried to kill a gopher a student had found. Unsure of how to kill a gopher, they took it into their utility closet, put it in a bucket, and began to hose it down with Misty Gum Remover, an aerosol that freezes gum so it can be broken off from whatever it is stuck to. Spraying away with the doors to the tiny room closed, one of the janitors thought it might be a good time to light a cigarette. Bad idea: the resulting explosion blew them all out of the closet. All three were hospitalized, and 16 nearby students received minor injuries from the blast. The gopher, which was not hurt, was later released into a field by police. (AP) ...*Moe, Curly and Larry are expected to survive.*

Bottle Baby
Test Tube Parents May be the Best, Study Finds
Reuter headline

16 April 1995

Decorated Eggs on their Faces: The Church of England's Easter advertising campaign featured a new slogan: "Surprise! said Jesus to his friends three days after they buried him." Gone is the cross, which "carries too much cultural baggage," said Rev. Robert Ellis of the church-owned Advertising Network, which produced the ads. The Church created the ad posters to bring in people who normally don't come to Easter services, and were not aimed at "the one or two theologically literate who could critique it," spokesman Rev. Martin Short said. (AP) *...True: He didn't shout "Surprise!", but "Boo!"*

I'll Get Back to You: Roland Brauwers, 42, volunteered to be crucified in an annual celebration of Good Friday in San Pedro Cutud, near Manila. However, the Belgian man backed out at the last minute, saying he hadn't had enough time to prepare for being nailed to a cross. Maybe next year, Brauwers says. (Reuter) *...That's ok, we'll wait — we don't get that many volunteers.*

Bailiff, Clear the Court: Officials at the Dade County Courthouse in Miami have to deal with many defendants who use sacrifices to try to gain advantage in court proceedings. To help deal with the results, a "Voodoo Squad" has been created to clear out charms and the bodies of dead chickens and goats each morning before court convenes. The problem has been blamed on the high number of Cubans and Haitians in court. (Reuter) *...Actually, court deputies have been using the grounds for nightly barbecue parties.*

Highest Bidder: Hamilton, Ohio, police allege that Clarence Wilkinson, 44, offered Chris Brown, 19, $12,500 to kill his former wife, Melissa Frances, 43. Then, police say, Brown struck a deal with Frances to kill Wilkinson for $15,500. Frances then changed her mind and asked for her money back. Brown refused the cancellation request, saying a further payment of $2,500 was required for him *not* to kill Wilkinson. Brown has pleaded guilty of extortion in the cancellation deal and faces 10 years. Wilkinson faces a minor charge of "inducing panic". Frances pleaded guilty to a reduced charge and has been sentenced to six months in jail and a $500 fine. So far, none of the trio face charges of conspiracy to commit murder. (AP) ...*Coming soon to a theater near you.*

Finders Keepers: A gang of thieves in London were dismayed to find that police had discovered and impounded their getaway car — with a stolen safe still inside. So they broke into the police station and stole the car back, their earlier haul still inside. To add insult to injury, the bad guys called a local newspaper to boast of their deed. "We [got] 13,000 pounds out of the job, and I am looking forward to a nice holiday. We made the Old Bill look [like] real idiots, it was so easy," they told the Daily Star. "The vehicle has now been recovered," a police spokesman noted, but "the safe was no longer in the boot." (Reuter) ...*Hah, the joke's on you: we changed the combination!*

Arrest that Snake: Brooklyn Heights, Ohio, police arrested Brian Dawson on traffic charges. While Dawson was changing into a jail uniform, a boa constrictor slid out of his underwear. Dawson insisted the snake was a pet that he was just trying to keep warm, but Peggy Alison, the owner of a pet store in nearby Parma, recognized the snake when it was shown on TV news as one stolen from her store. (AP) ...*Can't really blame it for diving for freedom once it got the chance.*

I Know Why The Caged Bird Sings: Tokyo police have a new tool in their arsenal against the cult suspected of nerve-gas attacks: caged canaries. The birds are carried on searches of suspected cult properties. However, after three weeks of work, the canaries are showing signs of extreme stress; one has pulled out many of its own feathers. "Maybe even the canaries are becoming tired after three weeks of this search," a police officer said. (Reuter) ...*A bird can hold its breath for only so long.*

Sail Away: Britain's Millennium Commission, trying to think up ways to celebrate the year 2000, is considering a proposal to launch 2000 one-pound coins into space, each propelled in a different direction by solar sails and steered by remote control. Anyone who finds and returns a coin would be eligible for a prize. "It could take centuries before they are all found," a spokesman said. The coins would encourage space exploration, the idea's sponsors say. (Reuter) *...To heck with finding new planets or discovering intelligent life. I could win a prize for finding a quid!*

A Long, Long Way
Spaniard Dies After Fall from Ferry to Britain
Reuter headline

---

23 April 1995 . . . .

All Aboard: Bob Dornan, a conservative republican who is running for President on a platform criticizing the country's "moral decay", is riding a train on a whistle-stop tour to tout his candidacy. At an unscheduled stop in Wilmington, Del., a man wearing a dress and wig greeting Dornan with a falsetto "Hi, Bobby!" led aides to shield him from the man. But Dornan recognized the drag queen as Thomas Carper, Delaware's Democratic governor, who was apparently in costume for a fund-raising skit. (AP) *...It really scared him: for a minute, he thought for sure it was his first wife.*

Last Supper: Animal rights activists were blocked from entering St. Peter's Square at the Vatican, where they planned a protest to prompt the Pope to encourage people to stop eating meat. The protestors, dressed as various farm animals, carried a banner reading "Killing is Wrong, Vegetarians Agree". (Reuter) *...There's no truth to the rumor that the Pope suggested they be fed to the lions.*

Lies, Damn Lies, and Statistics: An investigation by the Wall Street Journal shows that many U.S. universities give varying answers on surveys seeking information in order to rank the schools. For instance, Long Island University told U.S. News and World Report, which rates schools in a special annual issue, that its graduation rate is 55%, but told

the National Collegiate Athletic Association that the graduation rate is 28%. A spokeswoman for Wesleyan University
noted the top-ten lists are important aids in attracting
students. "It's a wonderful marketing tool for the school
ranked No. 1," she said. (AP) ...*And only a few schools can be
rated number 1, you know.*

Would You Like Fries With That? Dale Jones and Della
Johnston met at a McDonald's restaurant in Nashville,
Tenn. On Saturday, the restaurant closed for 20 minutes so
the couple could be married under its golden arches. The
restaurant also donated honeymoon clothes to the couple,
and promises to give them a free meal every year on their
anniversary. (AP) ...*Darling, you look so irresistible in your
brown polyester jumpsuit and paper hat.*

Groom's Family, Section B, Rows 18-46: Tracy Witak and
Matthew Ray were married at the Joe Louis Arena in
Detroit on the center ice just before a game between the
Detroit Red Wings and the Winnipeg Jets. With perfect
timing, they were pronounced married just as the opening
horn blew. There were 19,000 fans in the stands. (AP) ...*Hey:
illegal body check. Into the penalty box you go.*

I've Got a Fever: So many people are gambling so much
money on Great Britain's National Lottery that they are
neglecting other financial obligations. Like what? Spending on undertakers has dropped 11.1% since the lottery
began. (Reuter) ...*Maybe the lottery is just giving people a reason
to live.*

I Found It: Malcolm Macbeth owns a car wash across the
street from the Spirit of Life Catholic Church in Mandan,
N.D. An overflow of parishioners attending Easter mass
were parking on and walking across his lot to get to the
church. Fearing the extra cars would block customers, Macbeth hurried the churchgoers along by brandishing an
assault rifle. "I just lost it," Macbeth told a judge after his
arrest. "I'm concerned you might lose it again," the judge
replied. Macbeth faces a five-year sentence on felony
charges. (AP) ...*Malcolm, you need some rest. Take Sundays off
for a while.*

That Ain't Right: Donna Dowling, an English teacher at
Northwood Middle School in Greenville, S.C., noticed that
the slogan on her steak sauce bottle proclaimed "Its' unique

tangy blend of herbs and spices bring out the natural taste of steak." Her students wrote the Heinz company about the grammatical errors: there's no apostrophe in "its" and "bring" should be "brings", the students pointed out. Heinz promised to change the label: "As a result of your letters, the back label of 57 Sauce will be redesigned with new verbiage," spokeswoman Mary Katanick told the students in a letter. (AP) ...*I think I now know what the problem is.*

No Handsome Princes: To combat a drought, farmers in the Rangpur province of Bangladesh are catching frogs and marrying them to each other to encourage rain. Both Islamic and Hindu wedding ceremonies are being used, and the hitched croakers are then released back into the ponds where they were caught. "I've done it before and it worked," one farmer said. At least 12 frog wedding ceremonies have been performed in the region in recent days. (AP) ...*See, I told you it worked: it's raining cats and dogs.*

Cookbook: Police in West Milford, N.J., arrested two 12-year-old boys for making napalm and keeping it in their school lockers. It was not known what the boys were going to do with the jelled gasoline mixture. "I am not shocked," a police spokesman said, since "books that give directions on how to make napalm and other explosives [have been sold] for at least 15 years. These kids can read." (Reuter) ...*Are you sure? That would put them ahead of most other kids their age.*

The Guards Ate My Homework: Hagerstown, Md., Circuit Judge Daniel Moylan sentenced Ronald Wilson, 18, to five years in prison for his role in a drive-by shooting. The judge also ordered Wilson to read "The Ox Bow Incident" and write a report on the book. (AP) ...*That's it, your honor, throw the book at him!*

Don't We All?
Iceland Relies on Fish, Energy, Beauty to Stay Rich
Reuter headline

30 April 1995 . . . .

Damned Thief: A statue of a "land grandfather" god stolen from a Taoist temple in Taipei has been offered back for a $50,000 ransom. The thief also advised the temple not to contact the police. "What is he going to do, kill the god?" a temple spokesman said after calling the police anyway. He said the ransom would not be paid. "Hell, with $50,000 we can buy 10 gods." (Reuter) ...*And that's just the gift shop price. Wholesale, they're even cheaper.*

All Undressed, Nowhere to Go: Darlene Hendrickson, a Carson City, Nev., paralegal who has also worked as a prostitute in local brothels, picketed the state capitol in an attempt to get legislative support for a prostitutes' union. She says a union is needed because police don't take complaints of abuse by other brothel employees seriously, and support from the legislature would help keep brothels from firing workers who join. (AP) ...*But wouldn't collective bargaining be considered kinky?*

Mark Your Calendar: May 25 to 27, Hong Kong's Cultural Centre will host the International Symposium on Public Toilets. But that's not all: "As part of the symposium, the overseas visitors will be taken on a tour of some local toilets on May 27," an official announcement said. (Reuter) ...*Look, when I say I need to "visit a toilet," I mean now, not two days from now.*

Fish Story: Wayne Andrews, a sheriff deputy in Boulder, Colo., loved the vegetarian pizza at Pasta Jay, a Boulder restaurant, but could never figure out what the delicious secret ingredient in the sauce was. He recently found out: anchovies, which are against Andrews' diet prohibitions. Andrews sued the restaurant for misrepresentation, and was awarded $463.24, the cost of all the pizzas Andrews ate over the last five years. (AP) ...*Those **were** diet Cokes I washed those down with, right? Right?*

Bend Over if you Love Me: Paul Armstrong proposed to Connie Norman. The London man had "Connie will you marry me?" tattooed on his rear end, asked her to give him a massage, then waited until she found the question. Good thing she agreed. "I don't know what I'd have done if she gave me the bum's rush," Armstrong said. Norman plans to have "Yes" tattooed on her rear as a response. (Reuter) *...Very good sir. Would you like that in block, script, or braille?*

Simple: The tabloid TV show "American Journal" wanted to show how easy it is to buy the components of a bomb like the one used in Oklahoma City by renting two vans and anonymously trying to buy nitrate fertilizer. But a dealer in Hightstown, N.J., suspicious of city slickers buying fertilizer, refused to sell the men a ton and called police. Later, police in Carteret investigated two suspicious vans, found 500 lbs. of fertilizer, and hauled the two in for questioning. A computer check of the vans' license plates linked the duo to the earlier incident. "We were operating within the law to produce an investigative report on this issue of national importance," a senior producer explained. (AP) *...Let's hope they don't plan any shows on how easy it is to kidnap children from school yards.*

Miscast: Paul Fifield, 19, wants to be an actor. A friend, Kate Freeland, wants to be an artist. Freeland talked Fifield into letting her cast his body in plaster for a "Greek torso" sculpture. Unfortunately, she used hard-setting wall plaster by mistake. "Kate was reading a book on how to do it, but I don't think she had got further than the preface," Fifield said. Doctors chipped the plaster away with hammers. (Reuter) *...For this actor, losing a part could scar him for life.*

Charge It: Eli Broad, owner of a California construction firm, purchased a Roy Lichtenstein painting at Sotheby's for $2.5 million. He paid the tab with his American Express platinum card. "I want the frequent flier miles," Broad explained — each dollar charged on his card earns him a "mile". The transaction, a record for American Express, earned Broad enough credits for about $40,000 worth of airline tickets. (Forbes) *...He's not rich because he's stupid: he also gets 30 days to pay.*

The Inexorable March of Science: New Scientist magazine reports that "NASA researchers" have given various drugs to spiders to see how they affect the arachnids' webmaking abilities. For instance, spiders under the influence of speed spin webs "with great gusto, but apparently without much planning, leaving large holes." Spiders given chloral hydrate, a sleeping drug, "drop off before they even get started." And on marijuana, they lose concentration and stop web-building half-way through. (Reuter) ...*Hey man, I'll finish if you'll feed me a few dozen flies first.*

Halt in the Name of the Law: An Israeli policeman sitting on a public toilet on the Temple Mount in East Jerusalem lost his gun when an unknown thief reached under the stall wall, grabbed the gun off the belt of his pants, and ran. The cop, who was not exactly in a position to give immediate chase, was unable to apprehend the thief. (Reuter) ...*Maybe an informant can help flush the bad guy out.*

Next Week, Indictments for Bacteria Murder
Eating Worms is Cruel to Animals, Activists Say
Reuter headline

---

7 May 1995 . . . .

I'm Not Addicted, I can Stop at Any Time: Shell Oil Co. has installed TV screens on gasoline pumps in some U.S. areas to show advertising for Shell products, but some gas station owners have changed the channel. One owner noted her customers "don't want to be bombarded with advertisements," so she now shows "CNN, a travel channel and cartoons." The screen only works while the pump is in use. (AP) ...*Hey, buddy: mind if I fill up your car? My tank is full, and I want to see the rest of this.*

My Daughter has a What? Roberta Cremonini gave birth to a daughter at a Rome hospital, and breast-fed the infant for her three-day hospital stay. But when she took her daughter home and changed the baby's diaper for the first time, she was shocked: the baby was a boy. An investigation discovered that hospital nurses had accidentally switched identification bracelets with another child shortly after the birth of the children. Both babies are back with their correct mothers. (Reuter) ...*Maybe the nurses need better lighting in the newborn changing area.*

Ah, There's the Rub: Pasquale D'Onofrio, 43, failed to return to the state prison in Enfield, Conn., after a weekend furlough. The Connecticut Fugitive Task Force quickly tracked him down to a friend's house, where he was found hiding in the bathtub. He was arrested and returned to Enfield to complete his 10-year sentence. The charge in that case? Prison escape. (AP) ...*Some people just don't know when to quit and try a new profession.*

Nothing. Try the Maid's Outfit Again: The London Zoo can't get their pandas to mate. Perhaps, Prince Philip noted, it's because they only see zoo keepers, and thus can't recognize their mates. So "I suggested they ought to put the panda into a keeper's uniform," the prince said. The zoo has apparently not taken the suggestion. (Reuter) ...*Maybe they simply need glasses.*

Hey, If You're Not Busy: Jeff Shrouds was flying from Minneapolis to San Francisco with his girlfriend on a Northwest Airlines plane when the cabin started filling with smoke. "This looked pretty serious so I thought 'do it now,'" Shrouds said, explaining why he chose that moment to ask his girlfriend to marry him. "I thought the captain could marry us on the way down if we were going to crash," Shrouds explained. The plane landed safely; the problem was traced to an overheated air conditioner. His girlfriend, Jody Nichols, accepted the proposal. (AP) ...*If you think that would have been a quick wedding, consider the honeymoon.*

Full Moon: Independent Television (England) weather reporter Fred Talbot was doing a live segment from the Liverpool Docks in front of a large map when a naked man jumped into the picture and ran around on the map. The man first ran from England to Wales, but fell off the map — and into the water next to the dock — trying to jump from Scotland to Northern Ireland. "He told us he had done it because it was a sunny day and it was a bit of fun," Richard Maddeley, the show's host, said after interviewing the man. "Anyone who fails to see the funny side needs a sense-of-humor transplant." (AP) ...*Mr. Maddeley didn't say which side he thought was more funny.*

Physician, Faith Heal Thyself: Bashari Abdelmoneim Saleh, 38, is a well-known faith healer in Khartoum, Sudan. But police, suspicious of his methods, asked him to perform his cures on television. Apparently, his methods didn't work out too well: after reviewing the show, a public order court sentenced Saleh to three months in jail and 25 lashes with a rattan cane. (Reuter) ...*TV critics in the U.S. are salivating over the very idea.*

Finger-Lickin' Good: Researchers at the Savannah River (S.C.) Ecology Laboratory have suggested how low-level nuclear waste at weapons sites might be cleaned up: feed it to chickens. The chickens' high metabolism burns off the waste, the researchers say, and after removal from the site and feeding the chickens non-contaminated food for 10 days, any leftover radiation in their bodies is eliminated. Would the meat sell? "If that meat is cheaper and you call it radioactively cleaned meat and you put it on the shelf for half price, I bet people in this country would eat it," one of the researchers claims. (AP) ...*They forgot the number one sales point: it's meat that cooks itself!*

I Can Dig It: Science fiction writer Brian Aldiss returned to his boarding school grounds in West Buckland, England, and, with the help of some current students and a metal detector, found a cache of his early stories. He had buried them in 1942 so they wouldn't be seen by his teachers — "Most schoolboys are obsessed with sex and some of the tales were full of erotic activities, though tame by today's standards," he said. He was 16 at the time, and charged classmates one pence to read each story. "They were eagerly received and avidly read by everyone in my dorm," he recalled. (Reuter) ...*Kids today can't relate, considering the nice data encryption programs on their laptops.*

What Was Your First Clue? A new municipal building in Yakima, Wash., has a small problem: the contractor apparently forgot to hook the building's toilets to the sewer line. It took nearly a year, but all of the pipes eventually filled up, and "the toilets all exploded," said Dick Zais, the city manager. "Right away you can tell something is wrong when stuff starts coming out of the floor drain," the astute public works director noted. The building is the new headquarters for the city's Public Works department. (AP) ...*Now: about that lightning rod connected to the mainframe.*

Sheep Dip Affects Farmers' Brains, Study Finds
Reuter headline

14 May 1995 . . . .

Choosy Bombers Choose Ryder: An elderly Chicago woman who noticed a rental truck parked on her street feared it contained a bomb, so she called police. Police didn't find a bomb in the truck, but did find 500 pounds of marijuana and 810 kilograms of uncut cocaine. Investigators estimated the street value of the haul was at least a quarter of a billion dollars. (AP) *...Either way, that was gonna be one big blow.*

Money Fever: Six men have been arrested after an attempt to pull off "the biggest cash robbery in British criminal history" by cutting open an armored van with a blow torch. "They managed to open up the van like a can of pilchards [sardines], but they also produced a horrendously expensive bonfire," the prosecuting lawyer said, estimating that 1–1.5 million pounds in cash was burned, set off by the "several thousand degrees Centigrade" cutting tool. The resulting column of smoke was so thick that "the gang panicked and ran away." The van held a total of 11.4 million pounds (US$18.2 million) in cash. (Reuter) *...After 20–40 years, the six will be quite familiar with the sensation of being in a can of pilchards.*

Money Fever II: Police say that Madeline Vasquez, 37, the Parent-Teacher Association president of Public School 10 in Harlem, has admitted that she set fire to the principal's desk in order to cover up her theft of $800 from the school yearbook fund. She apparently resorted to the fire after her plan to clear the office by calling in a bomb threat didn't work. Charged with arson, Vasquez faces 8–25 years in prison. (AP) *...What is it with people these days? No one knows how to call in effective bomb threats anymore.*

I'm Gonna Sit Right Down and Write Me a Letter: Residents of Clarksburg, W.Va., are in an uproar over letters mailed to them by J.T. Colfax, a janitor who lives in a boarding house in New York City. Since December, Colfax has sent about 300 letters, addressed to names drawn from the phone book, that are "a huge mix of everything, completely mundane details of what I bought at the store today to going out and having sex and how that went," Colfax says, adding that his campaign is a "literary project" meant to ease his loneliness and to help to "introduce homosexuality to small-town America." He intends to finish his "project" this December, but in the meantime, "Clarksburg can survive me," he says, "so stop hacking at me you bucktoothed, overall-wearing, inbreeding clowns." (AP) ...*Yeah.*

Celestial Christening: British astronomers studying how stars are born have detected a cloud of pure alcohol near the constellation Aquila, about 10,000 light years from Earth. The cloud contains the equivalent alcohol content of 400 trillion trillion pints of beer. "It seems the ethanol molecule is found in relatively high concentrations in regions where stars are forming," an American researcher said. (Washington Post) ...*More proof that it's natural to toast a newborn.*

Pop a Wheelie: The city of Bellevue, Washington, is trying to force the strip club Papagayo's Cantina to make its stage wheelchair accessible so that disabled dancers can reach the stage, which is currently accessible only via stairs. "It's just asinine. If you can't dance, why should you even be on stage?" asks a talent scout for Papagayo's. But Wayne Tanaka of the city's cultural diversity task force, which also looks into Americans With Disabilities Act issues, disagrees. "It's hard for me to picture somebody in a wheelchair doing what those performers are doing," he said. But "for all I know, maybe somebody would want to do that. It would surprise me, but we live in amazing times." (AP) ...*Hey: people in wheelchairs can be sexy too.*

Null and Void: An election official in the Philippines is attempting to disqualify all of the candidates for the Philippine Senate because all had illegally posted their campaign posters on utility poles. "The posters cannot attach themselves to the electric posts. They cannot materialize from thin air," Regalado Maambong of the Commission on Elections said. Do the candidates have any way out of the mess? "Maybe the best defense for them is that the posting is a miracle," Maambong said. (Reuter) ...*Great: now we'll have politicians claiming divine providence.*

Don't Call Us, We'll Call You: The robber of a restaurant in Pittsburgh was easy to identify because, before he grabbed the cash from the register and ran, he filled in an application for a job at the eatery — using his real name and address. (AP) ...*He knew he wouldn't get the job since the interview didn't go well.*

Not at the Same Time, Though: James Hewitt, a former British military officer who revealed last year that he had an affair with Princess Diana, said in an interview that he cannot find a job now that he has resigned from the army. "I'm only good at two things, horses and sex," he said. "I suppose that makes me unemployable, doesn't it?" (Reuter) ...*Depends on where you apply.*

Call Me an Ambulance

One in Three British Men Ready to Give Birth —Poll

Reuter headline

---

21 May 1995 . . . .

Forced Entry: In the middle of the night, Ron Hallam thought he heard a noise. Then one of his Brockton, Mass., neighbors phoned, asking "Do you know there's a police cruiser in your living room?" State trooper Paul Halpin had been patrolling when, he said, he had a coughing fit. He lost control of his cruiser, which blasted into Hallam's house. "I think Governor Weld should pay for this," Halpin said as he surveyed the damage. (Boston Globe) ...*Why should he? He hasn't paid for any of the other damage done in the state.*

Can I Take That For You? Two men who cleared several piles of iron from the Sangmyung Women's University in Seoul have been charged with burglary: it seems what they thought was scrap had actually been four sculptures, which university officials valued at US$45,000. "I can hardly believe these were artistic works," one of the men said. "I thought the school authorities were too lazy to dispose of them." The men sold the iron to recyclers for $27. (Reuter) ...*Obviously, they've never seen the paintings in the library.*

Shoulda Seen the One that Got Away: A truck transporting 4,000 pounds of catfish from a Maryland hatchery to a fishing lake in Chesapeake, W.Va., lost its load on the highway after a minor collision. Fire fighters worked to contain the floppers in puddles, but "they were on the road. They were on the ditch line. There were fish 100 feet or more down the interstate," a sheriff deputy said. Unsure what else to do, authorities donated the fish to local homeless shelters. (AP) ...*Funny, my "Road Kill Cookbook" doesn't happen to have a chapter on fish.*

Use a Creamer, Go to Jail: Carl Rankin, 35, has been charged in the robbery of a 7-Eleven store in Hamilton, N.J. Rankin allegedly filled a cup at the store's coffee stand, then used the coffee as a weapon as he grabbed cash from the register. But the clerk ducked when the scalding liquid was thrown, and was able to chase down the robber when he ran. (AP) ...*Careful, he might have a thermos for reloads.*

Pardon Moi: Believing tradition will hold, drivers in France are apparently throwing caution to the wind. Since 1965, each new French president has pardoned citizens of their minor traffic offenses. As this year's election neared, the rate of fatal accidents in France climbed — 16% in March alone. French insurance companies say this year's accident increase will cause 500-1000 deaths. The monetary damage is also significant: President Mitterand's pardon in 1988 cost the French treasury US$1.6 billion in unpaid fines. (Reuter) ...*Maybe it says something that the way to reach your constituency is to reward outlaws.*

Pardon Moi II: Meanwhile, in another traffic engineering experiment, the emirate of Ras al-Khaimah in the United Arab Emirates has found that the rate of traffic fatalities decreases when repeat traffic violators are given 50 lashes with a cane in the public square. Six weeks into the new practice, the usual one-a-week death rate has dropped to zero, and the injury rate has halved. (Reuter) ...*Reuter did not clarify whether the caning victims were included in the injury rate figures.*

Honey, I Divided the Kids: El Paso County (Colo.) District Judge John Hall has to decide a three-way battle for custody of twin girls. DNA tests prove that the 8-month-old fraternal twins have two fathers: their mother's estranged husband, and her boyfriend. Twins with different fathers are extremely rare, says Dr. Bradley Hurst of the University of Colorado Health Sciences Center. "I can't imagine there can be more than five or 10 cases reported in the medical literature over the last 100 years." (AP) ...*Maybe that's because no one could prove it until recently.*

Super Slide: Police from both cities are investigating a "rampage" of New York police officers attending a ceremony in Washington, D.C. Among other allegations, NYPD officers staying at the Hyatt Regency hotel were said to have gotten drunk while in uniform, pulled fire alarms, harassed guests, and, according to a hotel employee: "They took off all their clothes ...and went sliding down the [lobby's] escalator," which was slicked down with beer. "It was not normal." (Washington Post) ...*Yeah: normally they ride on their riot shields when they do that.*

Autopilot: The Anglican Bishop of Edinburgh, Richard Holloway, wants you to know he understands. "God knew when he made us that he has given us a built-in sex drive to go out and sow our seeds," he said in a recent speech. "He has given us promiscuous genes," he continued, and "I think it would be wrong for the church to condemn people who have followed their instincts." (Reuter) ...*Uh, Rich? Is there something in particular you want to get off your chest?*

Battle Zone: Principal Frank Lentvorsky of Scott Middle School in Hammond, Ind., cancelled plans for an "anti-violence walk" after two students were severely beaten in separate incidents. (AP) ...*It's ok to protest wrongdoings unless they're actually happening around you.*

I'm Late, I'm Late, Hold my Plane up at the Gate: An unidentified man who was apparently late for a flight from the Rome airport to Caracas allegedly used his cellular telephone to call in a bomb threat on the flight he was supposed to take, hoping that the delay caused by the search for the bomb would ground the plane long enough for him to get on. He drove the last few miles, found the plane still waiting, and got in line to check in. Meanwhile, police had traced the call to the cell phone and identified its owner, and pulled the culprit out of line. The man, who was charged and released, was allowed to board the plane, which departed about a half-hour late. (Reuter) *...Um, I think I'd like to cash in this ticket — I won't be returning after all.*

As if it Would Help
Union Factions Want New Heads
AP headline

---

28 May 1995 . . . .

Pushups: Hot on the trail of the "Wonderbra", which helps exaggerate the frontal charms of less-endowed women, comes "MiracleBoost Jeans". Special Spandex panels lift up women's rear ends to make them "rounder, better," says Michelyn Camen, spokeswoman for Sun Apparel. "This is the answer to many women's dreams," she said. A design for men will soon follow. (AP) *...Does the men's version enhance the back, or the front?*

Sometimes I Sit and Think, Other Times I Just Sit: This week 450 delegates from around the world gathered in Hong Kong for a conference on public toilets. It included an photographic exhibition of toilets from around the world by Ronald Leung Ding-bong, chairman of Hong Kong's Urban Council, who is more popularly known as "Dr. Toilet". But is an international conference necessary? "What goes up must come down. What goes in must come out," Chung Wah-nan, president of the Hong Kong Institute of Architects, told delegates. "It is what we do after it has come down or out that... deserves worldwide attention." (Reuter) *...There's a question to ponder: he'd rather be known as "Dr. Toilet" than "Dr. Ding-bong"?*

Chuck the Barberarian: Charles Gibson didn't like the looks of his Lakeland, Fla., barber, Charles Smith. "I looked into his eyes. He didn't look normal," Gibson said. "I told him, 'That's OK, I'll get my hair cut by somebody else.' That's when he revolted." First, Gibson says, Smith came at him with a straight razor. As the two struggled, Gibson says Smith bit his thumb off. "I told him, 'Look what you've done! Look what you've done!' Then he spit it out and ran away," Gibson said. Doctors were unable to reattach Gibson's thumb, and Smith has been charged with aggravated battery. The haircut would have cost $5. (AP) ...*If I had wanted a manicurist, I would have gone to one.*

Let's Play House: Lee Duncan was watching her niece play with her Barbie dolls, but the girl couldn't quite relate to them. The child said "nobody looks like Barbie," Duncan says, so she invented a doll to better match the styles she's seen around her home in Lismore, New South Wales. The result is "Feral Cheryl". So far, sales of the US$7.30 doll have been slow. "When they notice she has pierced nipples and pubic hair they do get a bit of a shock," Duncan said. The doll also features dreadlocks, tatoos and unshaven legs. (Reuter) ...*Well, if the kid can relate to **that**, she shouldn't have been playing with Barbie in the first place.*

Quicker sans Knickers: When Paul Berry heard a neighbor yell for help, he didn't hesitate: he ran out into his New Orleans street to lend aid. "It wasn't a pretty sight. You had me in my boxer shorts with my gut hanging out," Berry said when it was over. The neighbor needed help apprehending a man trying to break into a car. With his wife running after them carrying a pair of pants, Berry and his neighbor caught the suspect. But as Berry dressed, the bad guy escaped and had to be chased down again. "We were both so exhausted we just lay there and tried to catch our breath," he said. The unidentified suspect has been charged with burglary. (AP) ...*Or, "Pallid pantless paunchy patriarch Paul and partner pal pursue prowler down parkway; leaves pathetic parolee panting in paddywagon."*

Shhhhhhhh: Last Saturday night, Bangkok police raided a wife-swapping club which caters to wealthy married couples. "Several couples have become happier after coming here," says Chuchart Thanamongkolchai, a writer who runs the service. Police didn't have any problems with that — they raided the establishment because it was using loudspeakers after hours. (Reuter) *...I guess other couples have not become happier because they didn't come there.*

Shhhhhhhh II: California's governor Pete Wilson underwent surgery on his vocal cords about six weeks ago and has been prohibited by his doctors from speaking until they heal. It's cruel enough to keep a politician from talking, but Wilson is further inconvenienced since he is trying to run for president. But it's not getting Wilson down: he uses a legal pad to jot down notes to his aides, and has made several observations on the benefits of not speaking. "It's easier to express in one gesture to reporters what it used to take two or more words to convey," one note said. (LA Times) *...We need more politicians who understand that it's sometimes better to keep your mouth shut.*

Last Call: London brewer Young's stockholders will no longer be served all the beer and ale they can drink at shareholder meetings. Last year's meeting drew 650 owners, who guzzled 2,500 pints. Apparently, a fair number of people bought stock just so they could attend the annual meeting. (Reuter) *...They'll all just shift their money over to the London International Group.*

Ahoy There: Coastguard stations along Britain's east coast are on the lookout for Robert Turnbull, 50, who is sailing from Hastings to Dundee, Scotland — a 500 mile trip. In five weeks, he's had to be rescued by the coastguard seven times. Coastguard stations, who have nicknamed Turnbull "Captain Catastrophe", radio ahead to the next station to keep an eye on the hapless sailor as he passes from one jurisdiction to the next during his journey. (Reuter) *..."We find people fond of being sailors. I cannot account for that, any more than I can account for other strange perversions of imagination." —Samuel Johnson, 1759.*

All Extensions Assessed by the Inch
Kennewick Voters Approve Extension of Pubic Safety Tax
Tri-City (Wash.) Herald headline

4 June 1995 . . . .

Jurisprudence: James Oswald, 50, acted as his own attorney during his trial for a string of Wisconsin robberies in which a pursuing police officer was shot to death. Oswald suggested the judge order a "trial by combat," where he and one of the assassinated cop's sons would be given guns so they could each fight for their lives. The judge decided on a more conventional trial instead, where Oswald was found guilty and sentenced to 600 years in prison. (AP) ...*I can hardly wait to see what he has in mind for the appeal.*

Endangered Species: A fringe political party in Britain, the Monster Raving Loony Party, has been at least temporarily saved from bankruptcy by a bookie who didn't want to see the party go under. He said that the party's leader, known as Screaming Lord Sutch, "has given an awful lot of people a great deal of entertainment. It would be a shame to lose him." Sutch has run in — and lost — every parliamentary election since 1963. (Reuter) ...*The Brits are so unlike Americans. When raving loonies run for office here, we elect them.*

Pumping Iron: Debra DiCenso was arrested for trespassing because she refused to leave the men's side of the weight lifting room at a Boston gym. She argued that the weights on the women's side were not heavy enough — she can do curls with 65 pounds and leg presses with 600. The gym was segregated because women there didn't like to work out in front of men. "It's my constitutional right to work out with weights I can lift," she says. DiCenso, 29, is studying to be a lawyer. (AP) ...*You haven't taken the constitutional law class yet, have you Debra?*

Tall Tail: Peter Croke was playing golf in Porthcawl, Wales, when his tee shot on the 17th ended up wedged under the tail of a sheep that was grazing near the fairway. "The sheep looked mildly surprised by the whole thing, but we were in hysterics," Croke said. The ball still wedged in, the sheep meandered 30 yards closer to the hole, "then seemed to shake the ball free, like [it was] laying an egg," he said. Croke won the match. (Reuter) ...*That was a woolly good shot, Pete.*

Keep the Change: Seven men from New York have been arrested in Atlantic City, N.J., for passing counterfeit $100 bills. The men had passed $20,000 in homemade bills at five casinos without the cashiers noticing they were fake, but a hooker one of the men hired noticed that the three bills given her didn't look right, so she turned them into police. (AP) ...*It's easy to fool a company's employee, but never a company's proprietor.*

I'm Still Not Sure — Let's Check Again: Police and undercover officers of the Labour Council in Wesminster, England, are under fire for making visits to a massage parlor to see if it was operating legitimately. Nothing wrong with that, perhaps, except that it took 17 visits to make the determination, at a cost of 2,000 pounds for the "amateurish massages" they received. (Reuter) ...*You just can't get a good massage when you're wearing a bulletproof vest.*

A Peck of Trouble: NASA has postponed the launch of the space shuttle Discovery for a month. Discovery was to head into space Thursday to deliver a communications satellite, but woodpeckers have pecked at least 135 holes, some as large as four inches in diameter, in the foam insulation of the vehicle's gigantic fuel tank, making it unsafe to fly. But it isn't getting them down. "I consider this just one more rock in the road to success," Shuttle test director Al Sofge said. (AP) ...*This bark is tough to get through, but the sap you eventually get is outstanding!*

Bird Brains II: Asaad Liebig, an 11-year-old student in Concord, Calif., found a dazed baby hummingbird on the playground of his school. "It was sitting there, and it looked lonely, so I picked it up," he said. His teacher asked him to take it back outside, but before he could it flew onto his head and buried itself in his hair. It took school officials three hours to get it free. (AP) ...*I hope those teachers spend as much effort to get things into his head.*

School Daze II: According to a 1993 study of high school students, 25% of the girls and 10% of the boys say they've been sexually harassed by school faculty or staff. Another study, in North Carolina, revealed that 13.5% of the high school students there have had sex with a teacher. These statistics were reported last week as several high profile cases of teacher-student shenanigans came to light in New

York. "The city's school system is not a dating service for adults," a New York school official complained. (AP) *...Hey, buddy, don't tell us, tell the teachers.*

Major Hangup
Chatterbox Wife Murders Husband Who Hid Phone
Reuter headline

---

11 June 1995 . . . .

Next Window Please: A would-be bank robber in Jamestown, Pa., asked a teller to show him his safe deposit box, then demanded money when they got into the vault. When interrupted by the manager, the man panicked and ran out — but first he had to ask the manager where the door was, and then how to open it. "He had trouble with the latch, and she had to help him out," police said. Two hours later in Hermitage, 15 miles away, a man of the same description asked about a safe deposit box there and was directed to a teller. Instead, he walked up to a janitor and demanded to be given two cases sitting nearby. After the janitor told the man she didn't work there, he ran away again. The cases contained janitorial equipment. (AP) *...It's sad when people think they can just skip the apprentice stage and try go to work as a professional.*

Phone Home: The Search for Extraterrestrial Intelligence project, wrapping up the use of the giant radiotelescope dish in Parkes, Australia, has been hampered by closer-to-home signals. "We can tell when it's dinnertime," SETI researcher Peter Backus notes; the super-sensitive dish can hear Earth-bound microwave ovens. Cellular telephones and satellites passing overhead have also drowned out any possible intelligent ET signals. But Backus thinks a signal will eventually be found — "It's difficult to believe that we are the only intelligent species in the galaxy, given the billions of stars out there," he says. (Reuter) *...But they won't be too likely to stay if we offer them unevenly warmed frozen dinners.*

No, Really: "It is a tulip and nothing more," insists Dial Corp. spokeswoman Nancy Dedera. She's been saying that a lot lately, since the rumors have started flying. It seems many people looking at the can of Renuzit Fresh Cut Flower air freshener see a penis amid the flowers on the label. The company is changing the can design. (AP) ...*I didn't see it until I snorted the whole can — then I saw a lot of things that weren't there before.*

Bitty Winky II: The ecoactivist Greenpeace organization has taken a new tack on driving home the effects of environmental pollution with a new newspaper advertisement that has run in several British newspapers. The ad, headlined "You're not half the man your father was," shows a very tiny penis. "It's true," the ad continues. "Scientists have shown that some chemicals that we dump into our seas are causing willies to shrink in size." Further, sperm counts and sperm "quality" are decreasing. The result: "Now the human population is also at risk." (Australian AP) ...*Well, if everyone dies off, we won't have to worry about the environment anymore.*

Underground Economy: Burglars in New Delhi attempted to tunnel into a jewelry shop, but apparently got their measurements wrong: the tunnel terminated at a washing machine shop next door instead. Rather than leave empty handed, they stole a collection of religious statues kept in the shop. The tunnel was discovered by the washing machine shop's owner when he tracked down the source of a foul odor — the 15-foot tunnel led to the sewer system. (Reuter) ...*Yards, meters — what's the difference?*

Underground Economy II: A study by the Brit journal The Economist found that trash collectors do a better job of predicting the state of the economy than EC finance ministers. "The moral? The contents of dustbins could well be a useful leading economic indicator," the magazine concluded. (Reuter) ...*The more obvious moral is that the government shouldn't fuss with the economy.*

Zero Tolerance: A Providence, R.I., kindergarten student has been suspended for 10 days for bringing a knife to school — a table knife, which he brought to cut his morning cookie with. "It was on his person, not in his lunch bucket," the Pawtucket school superintendent retorted, defending the school district's "no weapons" policy. The six-year-old has no record of bad behavior and has a good academic record. (AP) *...Hell, if the punishment is the same, he may as well bring his Uzi next time.*

Mail Bomb: Tired of hearing how slow and inefficient their mail system is, Russian postal authorities demonstrated a new delivery system last week. They found there was some extra room on a missile carrying a German payload into space, so they loaded 1,270 letters into a special capsule on the rocket and dropped it off by parachute as it passed the Kamchatka Peninsula 20 minutes after launch. The landing site is nine time zones away from the launch site. (AP) *...Cross-continent, 20 minutes. Cross-town, 20 days. Either way, the cost of the stamp is the same.*

The Right Stuff: NASA employees at the Marshall Space Flight Center in Huntsville, Ala., are donating to a good cause. To test a wastewater reclamation system being designed for the space station, a urinal in the men's room drains into a collection jug. (There is no collection system in the women's restroom — all but a few have refused to participate in the study.) The urine is then processed, and all *...uh...* impurities are removed. All available water must be recycled on the station because there is no outside source for water in Earth orbit. And yes, the resulting water is used for drinking. "It's water. Water is water," says Charles Cooper, chief of Marshall's development test branch. "If you took a glass of tap water and decided where all that water came from, you might be more inclined to drink this water than that water," he said. One engineer who taste-tested the reclaimed water said it tastes "pretty good." (AP) *...Now now: no fair putting bourbon in it first.*

The Briterly Hillbillies
British Aristocrat Gives Guests Stewed Squirrel
Reuter headline

---

18 June 1995 . . . .

Get Yourself a Good Lawyer: Steven Welchons, 32, a public defender in Madison County, N.Y., is in trouble. Despite a good court record over his two-year career, it was recently discovered that Welchons not only has no license to practice law, he never even attended law school. The cases he lost — as many as 100 — may have to be reprosecuted since the defendants can claim inadequate representation, even though "his skills were at or above that which one would expect from someone two years in practice," the district attorney said. (AP) ...*This either says something great about Welchons, or something terrible about the D.A.*

Come for the Earthquakes, Stay for the Wildfires, Riots and Floods: Los Angeles has unveiled a new slogan — "Together, we're the best. Los Angeles" — as part of a $5 million campaign to promote economic growth in the region. It's "a slug of a slogan" sniffed Patricia Boucher, the owner of a Florida advertising company who submitted 75 slogans, none of which were chosen. She would have preferred, for instance, her own "Los Angeles is No. 1, one for all and all for one". Presumably, none of the 75 were as colorful as the gag slogan chosen by New York Mayor Rudolph Giuliani for his own city: "We Can Kick Your City's Ass". (AP) ...*Hey: you talkin' to me?*

God Save the Queen, or Whoever: Britain's Scouts threaten to stop pledging an oath to God and the monarchy after admissions of extramarital affairs made by Prince Charles. "When you look at the behavior of pop stars, footballers, some members of the Royal family or whoever, young people can be confused," a Scout spokesman said. "It will be hard for some people to promise to do their duty to an adulterer," Chief Scout Garth Morrison affirmed. (Reuter) ...*Yes, let's teach all of tomorrow's leaders that if something is hard to do, it's worth not doing at all.*

Good Reception: Troy Hardin, 19, of Portland, Ore., turned around next to his car. The next thing he knew, the car's radio antenna — the little ball on the end and all — had rammed 3.5 inches up his nose, piercing into his brain and impaling his pituitary. He pulled himself loose and raced to the hospital. "He's lucky not to have wiped anything out," said Hardin's neurosurgeon. "It's the weirdest thing you've ever heard of," Hardin said after it was all over. (AP) ...*Kids these days. They'll try **anything** once.*

Keep an Eye on the Dog: Geoff Woods, 52, was at his Port Talbot, Wales, night club when he removed his glass eye to clean it. But Floyd, the club's mascot terrier, thought it looked pretty good and ate it. "I'll be watching Floyd's every movement until it reappears," Woods said. "After a good soak in disinfectant I can't see any reason why I can't wear it again." The blue eye is worth 600 pounds. (Reuter) ...*Oh, the things that I've seen....*

Beat the System: The Los Angeles Sheriff's Office has returned $20,000 worth of bondage equipment to Betty Davis, 60, taken during a raid of her home. The whips, chains, and other items are "just my play toys," Davis, a great-grandmother, says. She had been arrested for soliciting prostitution, but her lawyer says her services were therapeutic in nature and did not involve sex. Prosecutors refused to press charges for lack of evidence, and the tools of her trade were released to her. (AP) ...*The cops were just mad because she had better quality handcuffs.*

Now Hear This: The town crier of Chester, England, can rest easy: despite measurements that his voice is as loud as a pneumatic drill, Dave McGuire's voice is not too loud. So ruled the city council, responding to complaints by local shopkeepers. "You cannot have a quiet town crier. It is a contradiction in terms," said a council spokesman. McGuire's cries of "Oyez Oyez" are "noisier than a passing bus that registered 85 decibels but no noisier than pneumatic drills which have been measured at 100 decibels," the ruling said. (Reuter) ...*People in town love him. It's the people in the next town that are complaining.*

Oh, There it Is: Patricia Tanzi, 45, reported her Cadillac stolen in February, and collected $15,887 in compensation from her insurance company. But police recently found the car — stripped of valuable parts and buried in Tanzi's Carmel, N.Y., back yard. "I've never seen anyone go to the extremes that these people went to," Putnam County sheriff's investigator Michael Corrigan said. "It was a professional job, but we were more professional." Tanzi has been

142   *This is True*

charged with felony grand larceny and insurance fraud. Other arrests are expected, presumably including the operator of the heavy equipment used to bury the car. (AP) *...Keep digging around — maybe you can find Jimmy Hoffa.*

Big. Very, Very Big
Researchers: Violence Is Huge
AP headline

---

25 June 1995 . . . .

Bagged Lunch: A New Hampshire Fish and Game officer caught a man with 28 lobsters who was taking them home to be put in the freezer — where 508 of the shellfish were already being kept. It seems that the man, an employee at a Portsmouth power plant, had discovered that the plant's coolant water intake was sucking in lobsters; part of the man's job was to clean the filtering screen every four hours. He faces a $30,000 fine and a year in jail. (National Geographic) *...And, worse, his recipe for poached lobster and his drawn butter supply have been confiscated.*

Learn the Lesson: Charles Hayden of Pittsburgh was concerned because Chris, his 13-year-old son, was failing five subjects in school. So over an 11-week period, Hayden took Chris out of school during his study hall class and spent 110 hours tutoring him. The result: Chris passed the seventh grade — and Hayden is being prosecuted for "illegally" removing his son from school. "I'm just kind of dumbfounded," Hayden says, noting that teachers kept him up-to-date on lesson plans to aid his tutoring. But "other parents have to work with their children during the evening," retorts school superintendent C. Richard Nichols. If convicted, Hayden could be sentenced to a fine of $22 plus court costs. "There's a lot of brain tissue chasing me for $22," Hayden says. (AP) *...Chuck, they'd have to harvest 50 Pittsburgh school officials to get enough brain tissue to match you.*

L'Amour Lost: Brothels and sex shops in Australia have organized a boycott against French products as a protest to France's determination to continue testing nuclear weapons. For instance, "French-maid outfits and French knickers are being taken out of window displays" of sex shops, says The Eros Foundation, which lobbies for the Australian sex industry. "The industry is also undertaking a major review of language and terminology which paints the French as lovers and therefore peaceful," their statement said, including the term "French kiss". (Reuter) ...*Careful: renaming that to the "Down Under Kiss" might cause real confusion.*

Greasepaint Giveaway: Samuel M. Richardson, 20, a clown with the stage name of "Piggy" who performs with Circus Gatti, was arrested at the Walla Walla (Wash.) County Fairgrounds on charges of forgery and burglary. But deputies waited until after his performance — "We didn't want to ruin the kids' day," a detective said — before hauling him in. Jailers took mug shots both with and without his clown makeup "to kind of preserve the moment," a sheriff spokesman said. (AP) ...*Yeah, someday he'll look back on them and laugh — without making a sound.*

True Mortification: AT&T mailed information on their "True Rewards" program to 175,000 customers. But when patrons called the printed toll-free number to get details, they were greeted with "Are you ready to get naked? If you want hardcore, uncensored, explicit sex now, then come and — mmmmm — take it!" Apparently, a printing error substituted a phone sex number for AT&T's number. "People have been calling and expressing their dissatisfaction," an AT&T spokeswoman noted. But not everyone is dissatisfied: "It hasn't been bad for business," said a spokeswoman for Amtec Communications, the company that provides the phone sex service. (AP) ...*No, really: I'm just calling so I can get more frequent flyer miles.*

Free Speech: A graduating senior of the Sullivan County (N.Y.) Board of Cooperative Educational Services high school recited a poem at the adult General Equivalency Diploma graduation ceremony, but only after taking off her gown — revealing she wore nothing underneath. School officials did nothing to stop her: "We really didn't want to risk the spectacle of suited men hauling off a nude woman from the stage," a BOCES spokeswoman said. (UPI) ...*Not without requiring an admission fee, anyway.*

Student Driver: "I was at a stop sign when the guy with me said, 'Hey, there's a little kid driving that car!'," Colebrook (N.H.) police chief Mike Sielicki said. Sure enough, the car was being driven by a 7-year-old boy. Not wanting to scare the first grader, Sielicki followed the car for two blocks without using his siren, then walked up to the car's window when the car stopped at a busy intersection. "He looked at me and said, 'I was going to be late for school'," Sielicki said. The chief drove the boy back home and "on the way he asked if he could drive the cruiser." Karen Mercier, who found the boy's bicycle parked where her missing car had been, noted "if I see that bike again, I'm going to lock the car." (AP) ...*How will you unlock it, when the key's in the ignition?*

Yes, Dear: Mark Gardner, one of several people in a pool that won the largest-yet prize in Britain's lottery, $36 million, has a problem: his soon-to-be-ex-wife wants her share. "Our decree absolute has not come through yet so I am entitled to half," Kim Creswell says. Has her husband's new-found wealth changed her mind about the proceedings? "It is the same as before. He is a two-faced bastard," she said. (Reuter) ...*That's 'rich two-faced bastard' to you, doll.*

Longshot: Mark and Deborah Holmes of Texas bought an old picture frame for 50 cents, and later found it contained what looked like an original manuscript of Longfellow's "The Village Blacksmith" — a find, if authenticated, that would be worth about $10,000. Some Longfellow researchers judged it "almost certainly authentic," but it was recently found to be a mere copy of the original manuscript, which was donated to the Library of Congress in 1942. "Of course I'm disappointed," Mark Holmes said. But "if the original is housed in the Library of Congress, why [did it take] so long for anybody to come forth and say that?" (AP) ...*They needed time to figure out which one was the copy.*

Good Clean Fun: A judge in Bowling Green, Ohio, has put the kabosh on a new business there: a car wash where topless women would service the cars. Pending a hearing, the women must wear "a minimum of shorts and a halter top," the judge said in a temporary restraining order. But the order left Khalid Sayed, the business's co-owner, a bit confused. "I don't even know what halter tops are," he said. (AP) ...*It's a kind of cloth that gets transparent when wet. Glad I could help.*

Medicare: Bob Maund, 74, of Tenbury Wells, England, couldn't stand it anymore. His tooth was bothering him, yet he couldn't afford the 20 pounds it would cost to have it pulled. So he had a friend at a local pub pull it for him — but not until after taking a shot of whiskey for pain control. "It was agony for a second," Maund said, "But my mouth felt perfect again after they gave me a pint of mild as a mouthwash." His friend, who used a pair of pliers, "did a lovely job and I've just had the best night's sleep for months." (Reuter) ...*The bastards probably won't let you deduct the shot and mild as a medical expense, either.*

Med School Gets Rough
Doctor Execution Policy Debated
AP headline

• • •

Extra Headlines from Reuter . . . .

Banned Books
Britain Builds A Library From Hell
July 1994

• • •

And That Was Just the Preview
Mel Gibson Film Puts 500 in Hospital
July 1994

• • •

Apparently Already Had One
Romanian Burglar Takes
Car Alarm, Leaves Car
October, 1994

• • •

Beat Me! No!
Denmark Mulls Case of
Battered Masochist
November 1994

• • •

Just Can't Get Good Help Anymore
Lazy Japanese Men Blamed
for Falling Birth Rate
November 1994

• • •

What do you Mean by "Cold Day in Hell," Dear?
Conjugal Rights in the Afterlife?
January 1995

• • •

Don't Get Up
Hong Kong Buddha to get
Million Dollar Toilet
April 1995

• • •

It Doesn't Even Cook!
Man Marries Guitar,
Wife Thinks He's Crazy
May 1995

• • •

No, They Just Answer More Surveys
Rats Outnumber Britons,
Survey Shows
June 1995

• • •

Extra Headlines from AP . . . .

Tried it Already
Acupuncture Eyed For Addicts
July 1994

• • •

Where do Kids Learn to Breed Livestock These Days?
'Baywatch' Trick Saves Rabbit
August 1994

• • •

The Rivets Didn't Hold
Weld May Help Deadheads
September 1994

• • •

Worry-Free Days are Over
Nuke Bomb Plant Said Troubled
October 1994

• • •

This Lawsuit Stinks
Dad Sues Over Changing Table
December 1994

• • •

Stand Up Straight!
AP Corrects Elderly Explorer
January 1995

• • •

Yeah Yeah, Enough about his War Record Already
Clinton Huddles With Canadians
February 1995

• • •

Beats the Alternative
Group: Average American Aging
April 1995

• • •

Huh
Boat With Explosives, Blows Up
April 1995

• • •

Best Place For Them
Toxic Diapers Found In Wash.
May 1995

• • •

If I Lie, Let God Stri——
Priest Killed By Lightning
June 1995

• • •

Bulletproof Pants at the Cleaners

Policeman Shot In Basque Area

June 1995

• • • •

About the Author . . . .

Randy Cassingham has a university degree in journalism, but he could never quite deal with the concept of intruding upon people in disasters to ask "How do you *feel* about this?" Nor could he ever keep a straight face when presented with the outrageously silly situations that people tend to get themselves into that might make it into the "news". So, not counting brief stints as a writer and photographer on his school paper ("it doesn't count, it was a *long* time ago"), he has never been a reporter. Instead, he drove an ambulance in northern California (keeping a straight face most of the time), and since has been a search and rescue sheriff deputy, commercial photographer, writer, editor, publisher, process engineer, consultant, software designer, curmudgeon and staff jester for various projects and companies. He is single and currently lives in southern California. The tom, Clancy, keeps Randy's lap warm when he writes.

Get More of *This is True*™

The *This is True* compilations are a yearly event, gathering a full year of Randy Cassingham's *This is True* columns together, plus many more stories and headlines that never made it into the weekly columns! You can order through your favorite bookstore, or use this form to get them directly from us. Either way, be sure to "Get One for Every Bathroom in the House!"

• • •

☐ I need more. Please send me _____ copies of "Deputy Kills Man With Hammer" at $11.00 each plus $2.00 shipping. Only one $2.00 shipping charge is required per order, no matter how many copies are ordered. (U.S./Canada/APO/FPO only. Write or fax for shipping to other countries.)

☐ Please put me on the mailing list to get flyers on future compilations of *This is True.*

☐ Please send me a 3.5" disk copy of your computer software, *This is True* for Windows. I've enclosed $5.00.

☐ I'm desperate for a weekly *This is True* fix — e-mail me information on how to get it by e-mail.

☐ Your weekly *This is True* column isn't in any papers near me, and it should be. I'm sending you the names and addresses of the editors of some periodicals that should get with it.

• • •

☐ Check or Money Order enclosed

☐ Charge my: ☐ Visa, ☐ MasterCard, ☐ Discover

Card # _____-_____-_____-_____ (Expires ____/____)
For the protection of credit card users, the "ship-to" name must match the name on your credit card.

Name: _____

Address: _____

City: _____ State: _____

Zip/Postal Code: _____ Country: _____

E-mail address: _____

Mail this form with check or credit card information to Freelance Communications, PO Box 91970, Pasadena CA 91109 USA, or **fax** with your credit card information to +1-500-442-TRUE.

Get More of *This is True*™

The *This is True* compilations are a yearly event, gathering a full year of Randy Cassingham's *This is True* columns together, plus many more stories and headlines that never made it into the weekly columns! You can order through your favorite bookstore, or use this form to get them directly from us. Either way, be sure to "Get One for Every Bathroom in the House!"

• • •

☐ I need more. Please send me _____ copies of "Deputy Kills Man With Hammer" at $11.00 each plus $2.00 shipping. Only one $2.00 shipping charge is required per order, no matter how many copies are ordered. (U.S./Canada/APO/FPO only. Write or fax for shipping to other countries.)

☐ Please put me on the mailing list to get flyers on future compilations of *This is True.*

☐ Please send me a 3.5" disk copy of your computer software, *This is True* for Windows. I've enclosed $5.00.

☐ I'm desperate for a weekly *This is True* fix — e-mail me information on how to get it by e-mail.

☐ Your weekly *This is True* column isn't in any papers near me, and it should be. I'm sending you the names and addresses of the editors of some periodicals that should get with it.

• • •

☐ Check or Money Order enclosed

☐ Charge my: ☐ Visa, ☐ MasterCard, ☐ Discover

Card # _____-_____-_____-_____ (Expires ____/____)

For the protection of credit card users, the "ship-to" name must match the name on your credit card.

Name: _____

Address: _____

City: _____ State: _____

Zip/Postal Code: _____ Country: _____

E-mail address: _____

Mail this form with check or credit card information to Freelance Communications, PO Box 91970, Pasadena CA 91109 USA, or **fax** with your credit card information to +1-500-442-TRUE.

Get More of *This is True*™

The *This is True* compilations are a yearly event, gathering a full year of Randy Cassingham's *This is True* columns together, plus many more stories and headlines that never made it into the weekly columns! You can order through your favorite bookstore, or use this form to get them directly from us. Either way, be sure to "Get One for Every Bathroom in the House!"

● ● ●

☐ I need more. Please send me _____ copies of "Deputy Kills Man With Hammer" at $11.00 each plus $2.00 shipping. Only one $2.00 shipping charge is required per order, no matter how many copies are ordered. (U.S./Canada/APO/FPO only. Write or fax for shipping to other countries.)

☐ Please put me on the mailing list to get flyers on future compilations of *This is True.*

☐ Please send me a 3.5" disk copy of your computer software, *This is True* for Windows. I've enclosed $5.00.

☐ I'm desperate for a weekly *This is True* fix — e-mail me information on how to get it by e-mail.

☐ Your weekly *This is True* column isn't in any papers near me, and it should be. I'm sending you the names and addresses of the editors of some periodicals that should get with it.

● ● ●

☐ Check or Money Order enclosed

☐ Charge my: ☐ Visa, ☐ MasterCard, ☐ Discover

Card # _____-_____-_____-_____ (Expires ____/____)

For the protection of credit card users, the "ship-to" name must match the name on your credit card.

Name: _____

Address: _____

City: _____ State: _____

Zip/Postal Code: _____ Country: _____

E-mail address: _____

Mail this form with check or credit card information to Freelance Communications, PO Box 91970, Pasadena CA 91109 USA, or **fax** with your credit card information to +1-500-442-TRUE.